Information Systems Engineering Library

Automating SSADM Projects

Including Guidance for Suppliers

LONDON: HMSO

Acknowledgements

Phil Lomax of Model Systems Ltd, under contract to CCTA, is acknowledged for the development of the original text. Paul Turner of BIS Information Systems Ltd, under contract to CCTA, is acknowledged for additional technical assistance.

© **Crown copyright 1994**   Applications for reproduction should be made to HMSO

ISBN: 0 11 330637 7

For further information regarding CCTA products please contact:

    CCTA Library
    Rosebery Court
    St Andrews Business Park
    Norwich
    NR7 0HS
    0603 704704

Foreword

The Information Systems Engineering Library provides guidance on managing and carrying out Information Systems Engineering activities. In the IS lifecycle, Information Systems Engineering takes place once the IS strategy has been defined. It is concerned with the development and ongoing improvement of information systems up to the operational stage, and their maintenance whilst in operational use.

The Information Systems Engineering Library complements other CCTA products, in particular the project management method, PRINCE, and the systems analysis and design method, SSADM.

Volumes in the Information Systems Engineering Library are of interest to varying levels of staff from IS directors to IS providers, helping them to improve the quality and productivity of their IS development work. Some volumes in this library should also be of interest to business managers, IS users and those involved in market testing, whose business operations depend on having effective IS support by means of Information Systems Engineering activities.

The Information Systems Engineering Library also complements other related CCTA publications particularly the Programme and Project Management Library, the Information Management Library for data management issues, the IT Infrastructure Library for operational issues and the IS Planning Subject Guides for strategic issues.

CCTA welcomes customer views on Information Systems Engineering Library publications. Please send your comments to:

Information Systems Engineering Group
Rosebery Court
St Andrews Business Park
NORWICH
NR7 0HS

Automating SSADM Projects

Contents

chapter		page
	Figures	7
1	**Introduction**	9
	1.1 Purpose of this volume	
	1.2 Who should read this volume	
	1.3 Assumed knowledge	
	1.4 Structure of this volume	
	1.5 Terminology	
2	**The SSADM practitioner and software tools**	11
	2.1 Introduction	
	2.2 CASE and application generators	
	2.3 Case tools	
	2.4 Application generators	
3	**CASE tools and SSADM products**	15
	3.1 Introduction	
	3.2 The nature of SSADM techniques	
	3.3 SSADM products suitable for CASE tool generation	
	3.4 Opportunities for the generation of SSADM products	
	3.5 Conclusions	
4	**Application generators and SSADM design**	61
	4.1 Introduction	
	4.2 The 3-schema specification architecture	
	4.3 Stereotype systems	
	4.4 Cut-over to application generator products	
	4.5 Implementing UPMs and EPMs: An SQL example	
	4.6 Supplier interface guides	
Annex A:	**The 3-schema specification architecture**	99
	Bibliography	105
	Glossary	107
	Index	111

Figures

Figure 1	EU-Rent case study: Logical Data Structure	22
Figure 2	Entity Life History for Rental Booking	24
Figure 3	EU-Rent case study: Entity Life History for Customer	25
Figure 4	EU-Rent case study: Entity Life History for Rental Day	26
Figure 5	EU-Rent case study: Entity Life History for Car Day	27
Figure 6	EU-Rent case study: Entity Life History for Car	28
Figure 7	EU-Rent case study: Entity Life History for Branch	29
Figure 8	Effect Correspondence Diagram: Precursor products and dependant products	30
Figure 9	Effect Correspondence Diagram up to Activity c	32
Figure 10	Completed Effect Correspondence Diagram for Customer Car Return	36
Figure 11	Update Process Models: Precursor products and dependant products	37
Figure 12	ECD with grouped effects	39
Figure 13	Update Process Model for Customer Car Return	42
Figure 14	Enquiry Access Paths: Precursor products and dependant products	46
Figure 15	Output layout for Branch Booking Enquiry	47
Figure 16	Required View for Branch Booking Enquiry	48
Figure 17	Enquiry Access Path for Branch Booking Enquiry	50
Figure 18	Enquiry Process Models: Precursor products and dependant products	50
Figure 19	Output data structure for Branch Booking Enquiry	52
Figure 20	Input and output structures with correspondences	54
Figure 21	Enquiry Process Model for Branch Booking Enquiry	56
Figure 22	EPM in the form of an Action Diagram	59
Figure 23	EPM in the form of schematic logic	60
Figure 24	An 80/20 rule	67
Figure 25	Implementation points in SSADM	70

Figure 26	Specification of enquiries in SSADM	78
Figure 27	Mapping of SQL onto the Universal Function Model	81
Figure 28	Update Process Model for Customer Car Return	85
Figure 29	Example update in COBOL ignoring UPM structure	87
Figure 30	Example update in COBOL using UPM structure	89
Figure 31	Example SQL enquiry	93
Figure 32	Enquiry Process Model for Maintenance Booking Enquiry	94
Figure 33	Checklist for Interface Guide	97
Figure A.1	A System Development Template	100
Figure A.2	SSADM Version 4 mapped to System Development Template	101

1 Introduction

1.1 Purpose of this volume

The purpose of this Information Systems Engineering (ISE) Library volume is to:

- encourage and assist suppliers of Computer-Aided Systems Engineering (CASE) tools to produce products that support SSADM practitioners more fully

- help application generator suppliers to provide guidance in the use of their products with SSADM Version 4 (hereafter referred to as SSADM).

1.2 Who should read this volume

The primary audience for this volume is:

- suppliers of CASE tools who wish to understand the potential for automating SSADM activities

- suppliers of application generators who wish to provide an interface between SSADM designs and their implementation products.

In addition, SSADM users who need to construct their own interface to a specific application generator – because no supplier developed interface is available – will find the guidance useful. It will also be of interest to SSADM users who have to validate interface guides produced by suppliers.

This volume is not directly concerned with the selection of application generators and CASE tools. The selection of tools is described in CCTA's Appraisal & Evaluation Library volumes entitled *Application Generator Environments* and *Case Tools*.

Readers interested in assessing the SSADM support characteristics of CASE tools are referred to the ISE Library volumes entitled *A Guide to the SSADM Version 4 Tools Conformance Scheme* and *Testing Criteria for the SSADM Version 4 Tools Conformance Scheme*.

1.3 Assumed knowledge

It is assumed that readers are familiar with SSADM, at least at the level of the ISEB certificates in SSADM analysis and SSADM design, and with the 3-schema specification architecture. (The 3-schema specification architecture is described in overview in section 4.2 and Annex A of this volume and in detail in the ISE Library Volume: *Customising SSADM*.)

1.4 Structure of this volume

Chapter 2   A brief overview of the SSADM practitioners' need for:

- CASE tools which support the generation of a full range of SSADM products

- guidance on how to customise the SSADM process model to make the most effective use of application generator products.

Chapter 3   Illustrates, by using a case study, the potential for extending the range of SSADM products that can be generated with the help of a CASE tool.

Chapter 4   Deals with SSADM design activities and their customisation when an application generator is to be used. The chapter also presents a specific example in which the database processes are to be implemented in SQL.

1.5 Terminology

The multiplicity and contradictory nature of the terminology used by vendors and in the press means that it is impossible to give a universally accepted definition of terms such as '4GL', '4GE', and 'application generator'. However, the advice given in this volume is directed at products capable of generating a wide variety of applications based on conventional database management systems (either relational or CODASYL). Typically such products contain a 'forms' interface; interactive query language; fourth generation language (eg SQL); report writer; data dictionary; database management system; decision support tools.

The generic term 'application generator' has been used in the text to describe products within this range, for reasons of etymology and consistency with other CCTA publications.

Chapter 2
The SSADM practitioner and software tools

2 The SSADM practitioner and software tools

2.1 Introduction

The productivity of SSADM practitioners can be greatly increased by the use of software tools that support an efficient and natural way of working throughout the process of developing an information system.

For instance, immediate productivity gains can be made by providing relatively simple facilities such as the ability to copy part of any diagram from one place to another, either within that diagram or into some other diagram. Practitioners should also be able to document ideas in any sequence they choose, and to select the moment at which these ideas are stored in the central repository. They should not be hindered by automatic verification checks – such as for unlabelled boxes and Data Flow Diagram (DFD) levelling – while sketching out ideas.

Real benefits for SSADM practitioners can also come from automating SSADM techniques, especially those that require little or no further fact-finding and require few or no decisions to be made as discussed in chapter 3. Other ways that tools can generally speed up the practitioner's work include:

- helping the practitioner with consistency and completeness checking

- providing navigation routes between SSADM's various specification products, eg moving from an entity on the Logical Data Model (LDM) directly to the Entity Life History (ELH) for that entity

- automatic generation of code from SSADM products

    - LDM to implemented database
    - LDM to Screen/Report Designs
    - Enquiry Access Path to SQL.

- tailoring to facilitate the automatic generation of code by an application generator, eg:

- modify the Enquiry and Update Process Models (EPM/UPM) operations to match those in the implementation environment
- replace EPMs/UPMs by operations and conditions on Enquiry Access Paths (EAPs) and Effect Correspondence Diagrams (ECDs)

• documenting SSADM products directly in the target implementation environment.

This volume gives a brief overview of the opportunities that exist for CASE tools and application generators to increase the effectiveness of SSADM practitioners by automating the creation of SSADM and implementation products.

2.2 CASE and application generators

CASE tools and application generators appear to be alternative approaches to supporting the development lifecycle with software tools. A CASE tool that provides effective support for the method can reduce development effort by generating many of the logical and physical design products automatically. Alternatively the use of an application generator may eliminate the need to produce some of the intermediate design products.

However, the separation between CASE tools and application generators is not clear-cut. Several of the most widely used application generators have a CASE tool front-end to support the design process. CASE tools which are capable of generating, for example, Update Process Models can obviously generate procedural language source code instead. The distinction is becoming increasingly blurred as both CASE tools and application generators increase their coverage of the system development lifecycle. Nevertheless, for most SSADM projects the current technology presents a choice between CASE tools, which provide effective support for the method, and tools that provide good code generation facilities. The tools that provide the best support for the SSADM analyst are not generally the same tools that provide the best facilities for generating a working system from a high-level description. This dichotomy should not exist: support for the production of well-defined requirements and for rapid implementation are both required by the SSADM practitioner.

2.3 CASE tools

SSADM is presented and documented in the SSADM Version 4 Reference Manual as an integrated set of standards. These identify which activities are to be undertaken, when and with what inter-dependencies; how the end products of those activities are developed; and how the results are recorded.

SSADM was developed on the assumption that most practitioners would use a CASE tool, and that CASE tools would evolve to generate or partially generate some products which were otherwise time-consuming for the analyst to develop. CCTA believe that this potential has not been fully realised although a wide variety of CASE tools currently support SSADM. What follows in Chapter 3 of this volume aims to encourage suppliers to invest in the production of such tools by illustrating how some of the most time consuming transformations can be automated.

2.4 Application generators

A primary strength of SSADM has always been that it separates the logical expression of requirements from the physical implementation of these requirements. In a third-generation programming environment the constraints of the implementation environment are only imposed in Stage 6 (Physical Design).

The situation is much less clear-cut with application generators. They provide significant productivity improvements by the use of stereotype system design components. The application of SSADM up to Stage 5 (Logical Design) without regard for the implementation environment is likely to result in a system design which cannot be easily mapped on to the stereotypes. To realise the recognised benefits of application generators, and avoid unnecessary duplication of specification effort, it is necessary to modify the application of SSADM before Stage 6.

SSADM, as described in the SSADM Version 4 Reference Manual, provides a development structure which is, and will remain, generic. The Structural Model is regarded as the default structure which is tailored to meet particular project needs. ISE Library volumes, including this one, explain particular customisations of SSADM for common project situations (eg using SSADM with an application package; rapid development methods; etc.)

This volume explains the customisation of the method if an application generator is being used to implement the design. However, the capabilities of application generators vary widely and different approaches will apply to different products. An efficient translation from SSADM products to implementation products relies on the later stages of the method being supported by more specific guidance. Providing product-specific guidance is the role of an interface guide.

Although some application generator interface guides have been produced informally by SSADM project teams, they are ideally produced by the product suppliers because a detailed knowledge of the product's capabilities is required. CCTA, in collaboration with the SSADM Design Authority Board, and the International SSADM Users Group Ltd, is encouraging suppliers to produce interfaces between their implementation products and the later stages of SSADM. Chapter 4 of this volume provides suppliers with an understanding of the issues that the interface guides need to address.

3 CASE tools and SSADM products

3.1 Introduction

This chapter aims to illustrate the potential for Computer-Aided System Engineering (CASE) tools to generate SSADM products, specifically:

- Effect Correspondence Diagrams (ECDs)

- Update Process Models (UPMs)

- Enquiry Access Paths (EAPs)

- Enquiry Process Models (EPMs).

ECDs and UPMs are particularly suitable: they are time-consuming for the analyst to produce and much of the process may be automated. EPMs require more analyst intervention in the production process than UPMs; but because the two process modelling techniques are so similar, EPMs could be added to the CASE tool 'menu' once UPM processing has been developed, for relatively little additional effort.

The intention is to supplement the step-by-step guidance within the SSADM Version 4 Reference Manual by:

- providing more detailed information on how to build SSADM products where appropriate

- highlighting issues specific to automatic product generation.

In the context of this chapter, generation means the creation by a CASE tool of one SSADM product type from other SSADM product types.

Step-by-step approach

For each SSADM product considered, a step-by-step description – following the approach used in the SSADM Version 4 Reference Manual – of the activities to be carried out in the production of the product is presented and is illustrated with examples from a case study. This precise approach need not, of course, be mimicked in the structure or sequence of the CASE tool processing. The guidance is intended to illustrate, primarily to CASE tools suppliers but also to SSADM users, the potential for product generation facilities rather than provide a full and detailed specification.

3.2 The nature of SSADM techniques

SSADM has been criticised for using too many techniques. However, the activities contained within the techniques are of fundamentally different types.

An ideal development environment would be one where the activities to develop the final design could be performed using the smallest number of techniques. However, effective universal techniques capable of fulfilling several roles are not available. (Prior to the development of the modelling techniques used in SSADM and equivalent methods, systems were specified using what may be regarded as universal techniques – eg flowcharts and descriptive text. A testimony to their effectiveness was the growth in the use of specialised modelling techniques.) Universal techniques can exist only at a level of abstraction – by generalisation – that makes them too general and unspecific to be helpful as a rigorous analytical technique.

SSADM techniques combine three elements: analysis, design and transformation in varying degrees:

- Analysis is concerned with discovering facts about the system

- Design is concerned with how the system is to be constructed from individual components; requiring the practitioner to use his judgement and make decisions based on facts and rules of thumb

- Transformation provides a detailed description of individual system components; using information from one or more SSADM products (or information identified using other techniques) to produce a more structured and detailed expression of the requirement. It is a re-expression of what is already known.

All SSADM techniques transform inputs into outputs. Those which require the discovery of new facts are regarded as analysis techniques. Those which require judgement and decisions are regarded as design

Chapter 3
Case tools and SSADM products

techniques. However, several SSADM techniques require little or no discovery or decision making. It is these techniques that are the best candidates for automation, and many are already supported in current CASE tools, although few tools support the full range of potential transformations.

3.3 SSADM products suitable for CASE tool generation

Clearly not all products may be generated automatically. However, the following transformations have already been mostly automated in current CASE tools claiming to support SSADM:

- building a set of normalised relations, from an I/O Structure

- building a partial Logical Data Model (LDM), from a set of normalised relations

- building a single LDM, from two or more partial LDMs

- building an Enquiry Access Path, from an LDM Required View

- building an Enquiry Process Model, from an Enquiry Access Path

- building an Effect Correspondence Diagram, from a set of Entity Life Histories (ELHs) and LDM

- building an Update Process Model, from a set of ELHs and LDM

- building a Physical Data Design, from a Logical Data Model and volumetrics.

The most appropriate products for a CASE tool to generate are those which are:

- based upon 'transformation techniques', principally a simple transformation of other products developed using predictable rules

- time-consuming for the analyst to develop.

Analyst productivity can be greatly increased with CASE tool support. Whilst few SSADM products may be completely generated by a CASE tool in every instance without analyst intervention, many mundane and time-consuming steps can be fully automated, leaving the analyst to carry out the remaining activities requiring knowledge, judgement or invention. In addition to being able to construct products more quickly, errors will be reduced, and transcription errors in particular can be eliminated. Moreover, some of the SSADM notations were chosen with the intention of supporting them with CASE tools, and there is likely to be a significant increase in project timescales if the products have to be developed without any form of computer support.

3.4 Opportunities for the generation of SSADM products

This chapter deliberately concentrates on the production of ECDs, UPMs, EAPs and EPMs. These are amongst the most time-consuming for analysts to develop, and are therefore critical techniques against which the effectiveness of CASE tools will be judged. Suppliers interested in automating some of the other transformation techniques, will find these well-documented in the SSADM Version 4 Reference Manual.

Before generation of ECDs, UPMs, EAPs and EPMs is discussed, some general issues and assumptions made in this chapter are outlined and the case study which underpins the discussion is described.

3.4.1 General issues and assumptions

There are a number of general issues and assumptions concerning automatic generation of process design products which should be noted before illustrating each process in turn.

Re-generation of existing diagrams

This chapter is concerned with the creation of SSADM products. However, once these products have been created, the CASE tool user may wish to amend them and related source products and then re-generate. For example, the generation of ECDs is likely to expose errors in the ELHs and the user may wish to amend the ECDs and the ELHs and then re-generate the ECDs. A problem arises for the CASE tool designer over what to do with the existing diagrams (which may have been enhanced by the user) when re-generating.

The CASE tool designer has (at least) five alternatives:

- to disallow regeneration

- to disallow amendment of generated products (impractical here since the CASE tool is not able to fully generate the products successfully in every case)

- to create another set of regenerated products, leaving the existing set of diagrams

- to overwrite the existing diagrams, thereby losing the user amendments

- to amend the existing diagrams, retaining the user amendments where they are consistent with regeneration.

Of these, the final alternative is perhaps the most desirable but also the most complex. This discussion is particularly relevant for EAPs and ECDs where there is more potential for user intervention. The problems arising from the re-generation of diagrams will be a familiar one to vendors with experience of developing software support tools; the purpose here is only to re-emphasise the potential problems concerned with regeneration.

Operations

In SSADM, and in this volume, operations are not shown to be associated with ECDs or EAPs. However, UPMs and EPMs may not be produced under certain circumstances, and in these circumstances operations need to be displayed on ECDs and EAPs. This should not cause significant difficulty to the CASE tool designer, since the operation data should be associated in the underlying design, with the appropriate enquiry access or effect.

State indicators

Each effect on an ELH has an exit value. These exit states may be allocated automatically by a CASE tool. Although it is legitimate to allocate each effect a unique value, UPMs can be simplified if state indicator values are optimised – update operations to set a state indicator

Automating SSADM Projects

to the same value as it was immediately prior to the event can be eliminated.

CASE tools may offer a facility not only automatically to allocate, but also to optimise, state indicators. This facility offers substantial productivity benefits to the user and the processing required is relatively straightforward. It can be summarised as: 'harmonise the state indicator exit values of effects that may (validly) be followed by the same set of effects'. To allocate optimised states:

- allocate values sequentially from left to right, starting at 1

- allocate a separate set of state indicator values to each set of effects under a parallel bar

- unify the states of effects which end options under a selection (unless those effects are iterated)

- unify the state before an iteration with that after each iterated component.

It should be noted that the state indicator may not be optimised for ELHs containing 'off-the-structure' structures and undisciplined quits.

The case study outlined in section 3.4.2 shows a set of ELHs with optimised states.

Blank effect boxes   SSADM allows ELHs to contain blank or null effects. These may be drawn where an effect is optional, with a selection of the effect and a null effect. These null effects cause problems when creating ECDs and UPMs, particularly when the process is automated – how can a 'null' event be implemented? The solution, which is always possible, is to redraw the ELH without the 'null' effect. CASE tool designers may wish to build in warning or error messages to discourage or stop the analyst from creating ELHs with null effects.

Automatability   The step-by-step approach below identifies which steps may be fully automated, which may be partially automated and which steps do not lend themselves to automation at all. Most diagrams do not require every step to be carried out, so there are many which can be completely and perfectly generated by machine. The remaining diagrams could still be generated but ideally with a warning of incompleteness; it should be possible to identify for the user the activities where work is still required.

An activity marked as partially automatable might be fully automatable if the user provided additional information to that which is normally included within the SSADM products used for generation. It is assumed here that the only information available to automate a step is that contained within the SSADM source products.

Similarly, some activities marked as partially automatable could be fully automatable if the CASE tool had a larger knowledge base and could exercise more 'judgement'. The CASE tool is assumed here to have only a limited level of 'intelligence'.

3.4.2 Case study background (LDS and ELHs)

A case study based on a car rental business, EU-Rent, has been developed to illustrate the guidance given. The example event, Customer Car Return, for which an ECD and a UPM are built, is fairly complex in order to illustrate a wide variety of steps (although it is not possible to choose an example that will effectively illustrate every activity).

Customer Car Return is the event where the customer returns the car safely to a Eu-Rent branch on the expected date. The return may be made to the issuing branch or a different branch. When a car is returned to a different branch to the issuing branch, the return branch becomes responsible for the car.

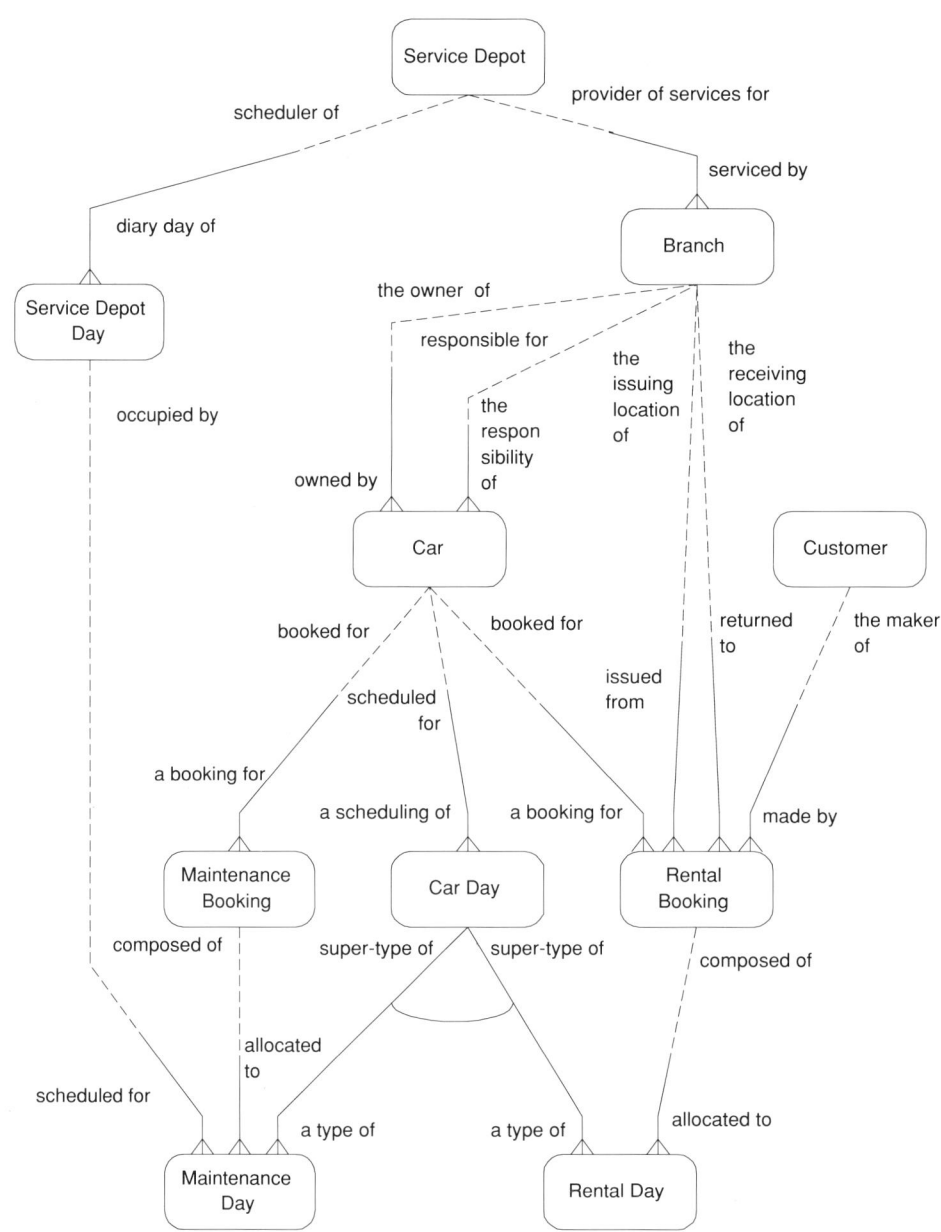

Figure 1: EU-Rent case study: Logical Data Structure

Chapter 3
Case tools and SSADM products

The Customer Car Return event causes the 'death' of a Rental Booking and a set of Rental Days. It also has a 'loss' effect on a Car entity and where the return Branch differs from the Branch that issued the Car, a new Branch (the return Branch) becomes responsible for the Car.

The Logical Data Structure (LDS) and relevant ELHs for the event Customer Car Return are at Figures 1 to 7.

As can be seen in Figure 1, the Car entity has two relationships to Branch: the Branch which purchased and therefore owns the Car and the Branch which is currently responsible for the Car. A Branch may be both responsible for, and the owner of, the Car. The responsible Branch is the one where the Car is located; when the car is on hire, it is the Branch which issued the Car.

Figure 1 also shows that the Rental Booking has two relationships to Branch: an issuing Branch and a return Branch, both of which may be the same. These are set at the time of booking and a Customer must return the car to the agreed Branch.

The Customer Car Return event therefore has no effect on the relationships between Rental Booking and Branch. However, where the return Branch differs from the issuing Branch, the return Branch becomes responsible for the Car and the relevant relationship from Car to Branch must be swapped.

The set of life histories shown below includes only those relevant to the Customer Car Return event, ie those in which Customer Car Return appears. The ELHs include state indicators which have been optimised and use only disciplined quits (shown as Q1, R1 etc). Each ELH is discussed briefly in terms of its relevance to the Customer Car Return event. To avoid extraneous detail the logical death event is taken to be physical death. No additional archiving or deletion events are assumed. This simplifies the example at the expense of some realism – for example, no history of rental bookings is maintained.

Automating SSADM Projects

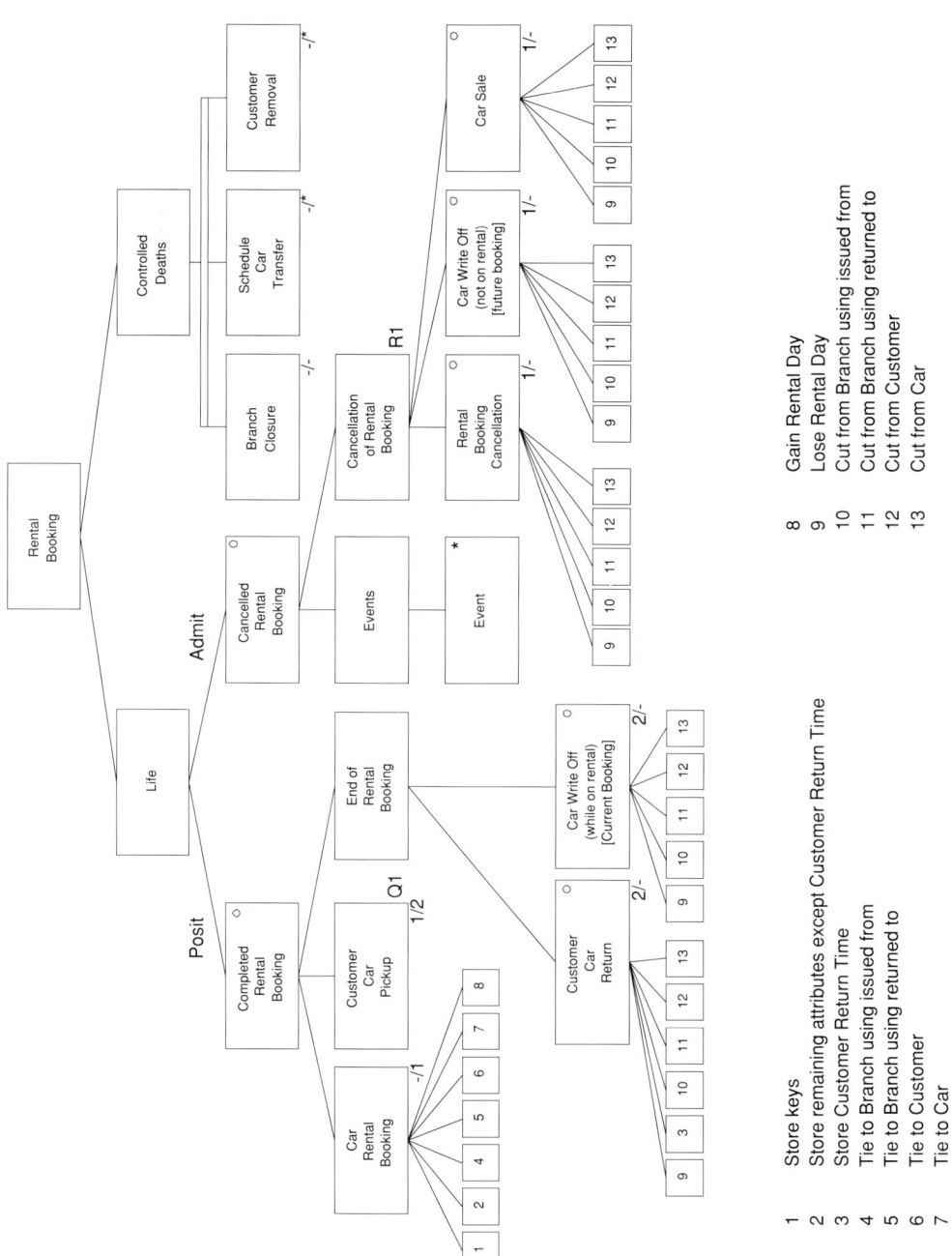

Figure 2: Entity Life History for Rental Booking

In Figure 2, the Customer Car Return event marks the normal end of a Rental Booking. The parallel bars at the end of the ELH for Rental Booking handle the 'controlled death' events (Branch Closure, Schedule Car Transfer, Customer Removal) which may not happen whilst there are 'live' Rental Bookings. These 'controlled death' events have no impact on the Customer Car Return event.

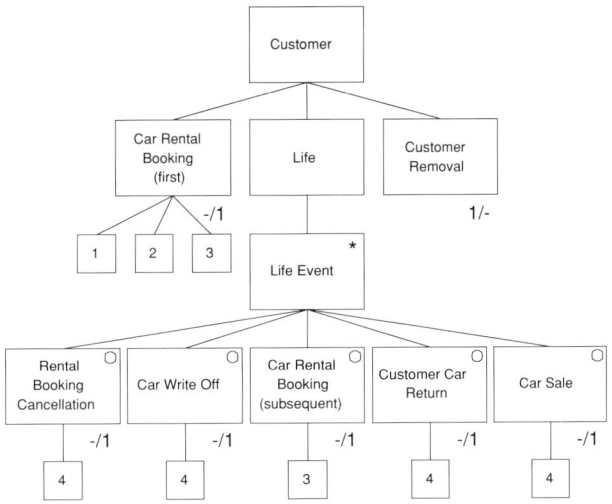

1. Store keys
2. Store remaining attributes
3. Gain Rental Booking
4. Lose Rental Booking

Figure 3: EU-Rent case study: Entity Life History for Customer

As shown in Figure 3, the Rental Booking 'dies' as a result of the event and this causes a 'loss' effect on Customer.

The 'death' of the Rental Booking also leads to the 'death' of a set of Rental Days as shown in Figure 4.

Each Rental Day is a type of Car Day and so Car Day also 'dies'. This is depicted in Figure 5.

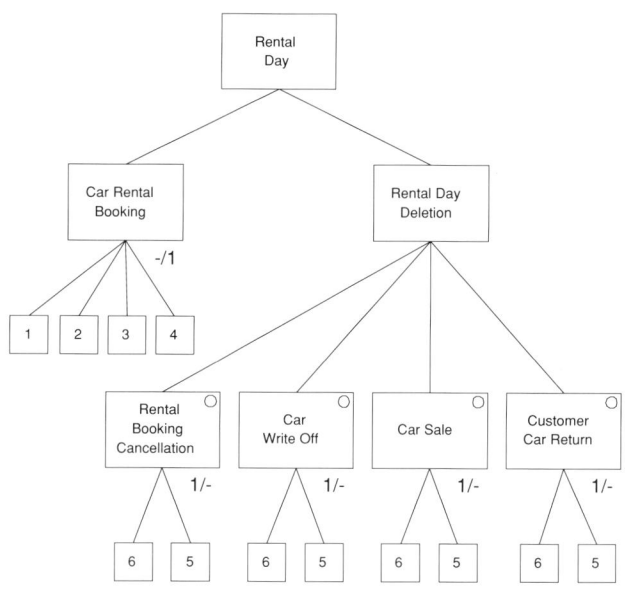

1	Store keys	4	Tie to Car Day
2	Store remaining attributes	5	Cut from Rental Booking
3	Tie to Rental Booking	6	Cut from Car Day

Figure 4: EU-Rent case study: Entity Life History for Rental Day

The 'death' of Rental booking also has a 'loss' effect on Car but, more significantly, if the Car is returned to a different Branch from the issuing Branch, the 'responsible for' relationship to Branch must be swapped. This can be seen in Figure 6.

Finally, as shown in Figure 7, if the Car is returned to a different Branch from the issuing Branch, another Branch 'gains' the Car and the existing one must 'lose' the Car. The event affects two instances of Branch – the existing Branch responsible and the newly responsible Branch.

Complexity has been avoided in Figure 7 by omitting the full effect structure beneath the events Car Write Off; Car Sale; Rental Booking Cancellation; Car Rental Booking. All of these events involve more than one relationship between a master Branch entity and a single detail entity.

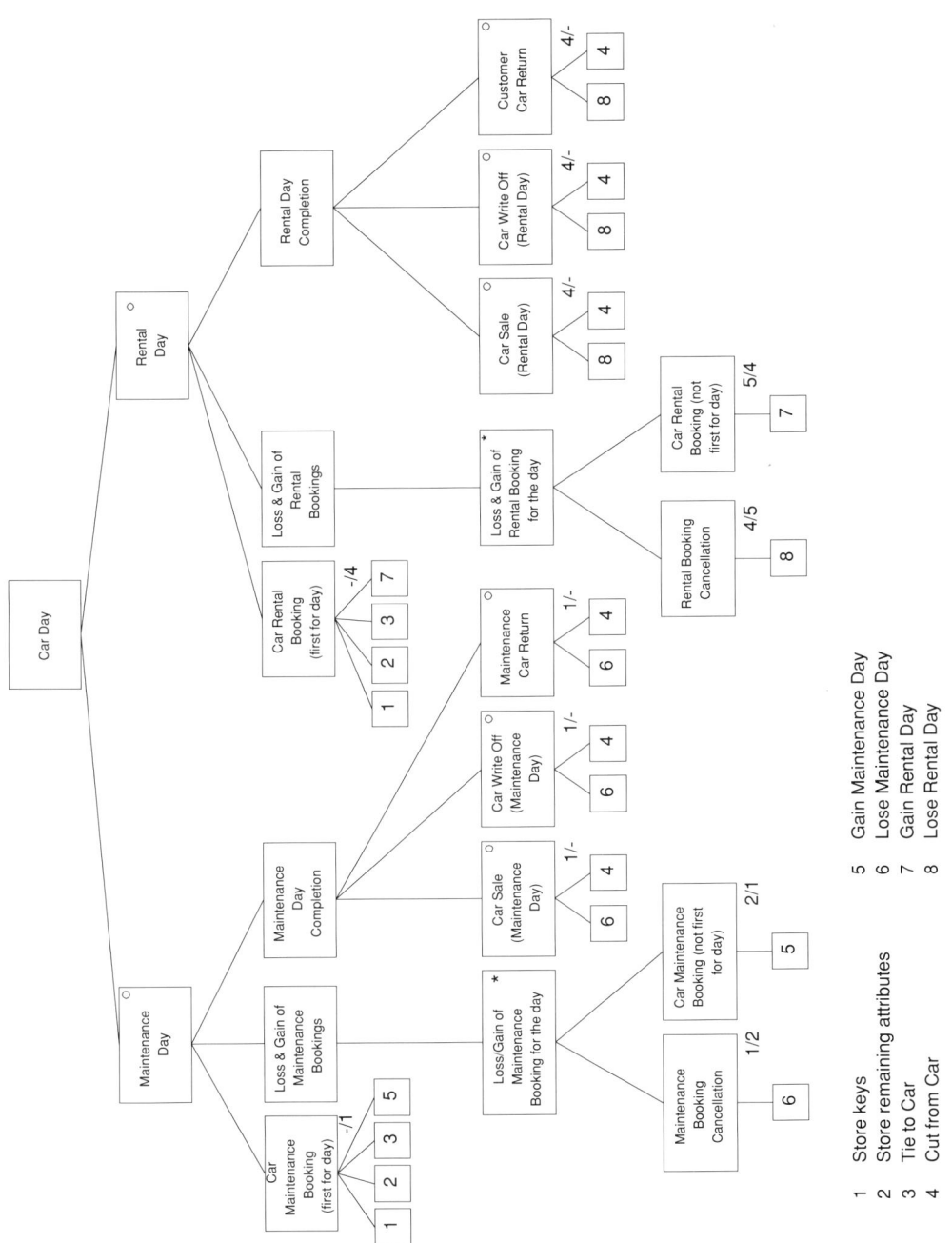

Figure 5: EU-Rent case study: Entity Life History for Car Day

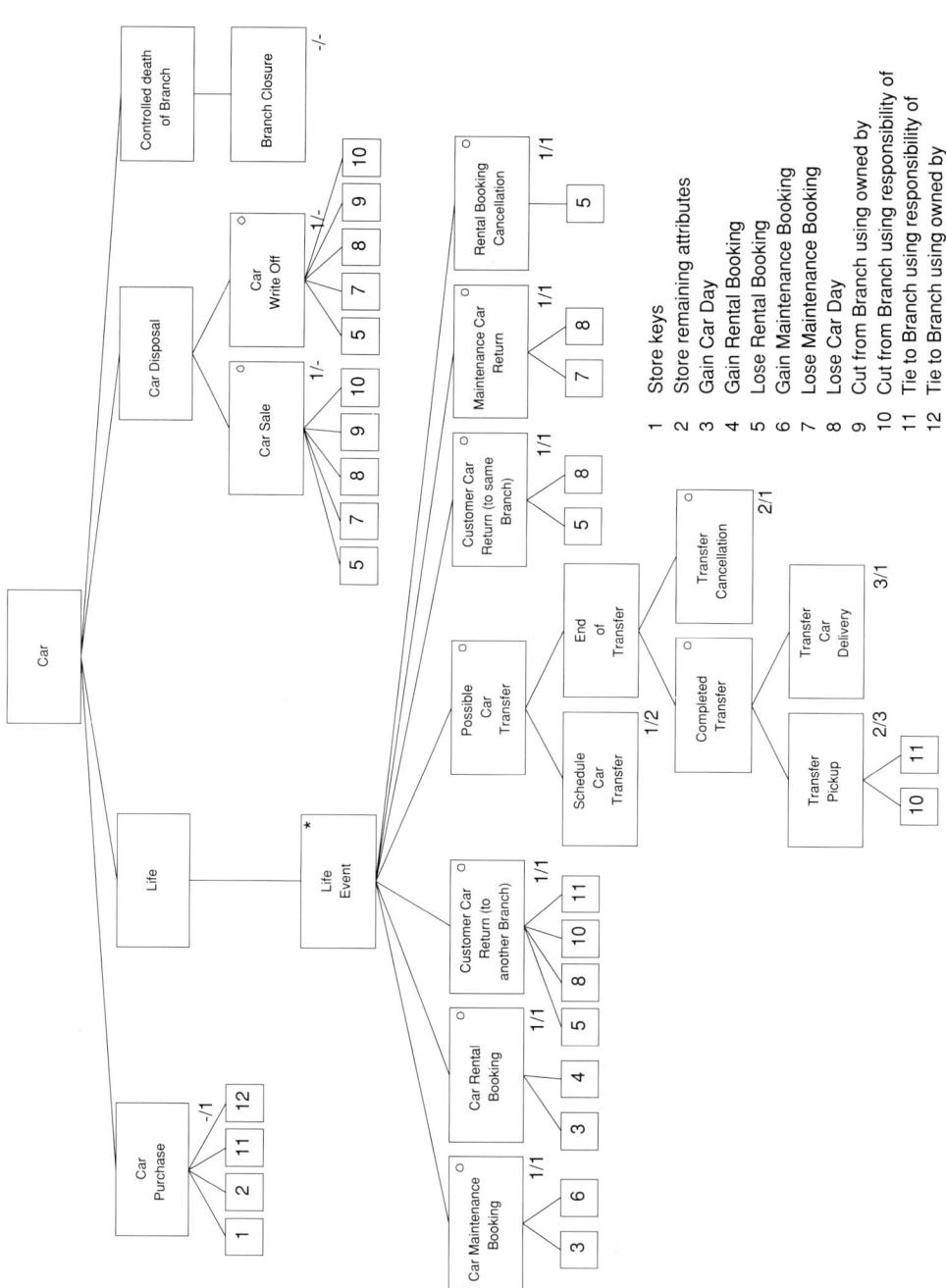

Figure 6: EU-Rent case study: Entity Life History for Car

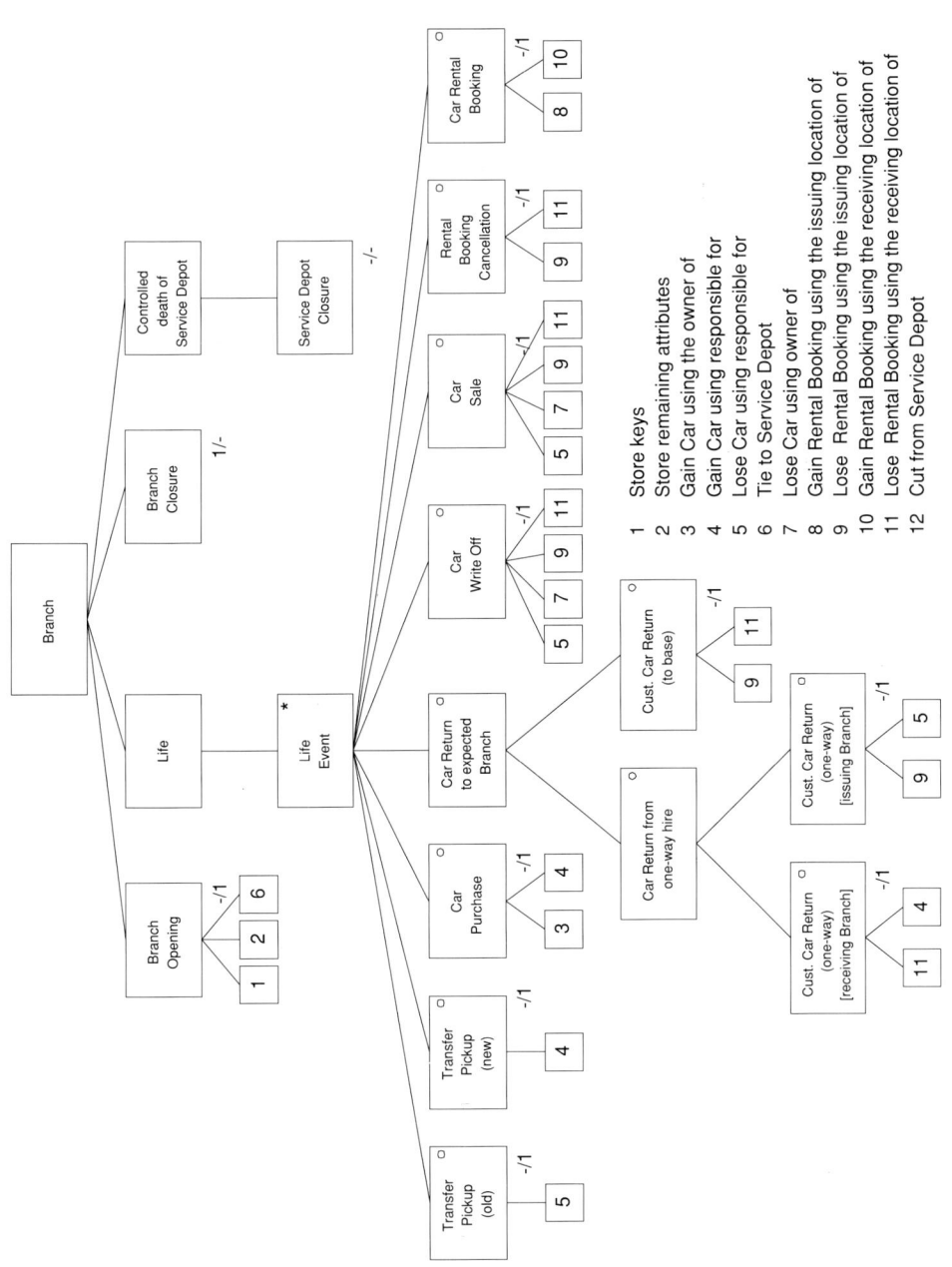

Figure 7: EU-Rent case study: Entity Life History for Branch

3.4.3 Generating Effect Correspondence Diagrams (ECDs)

The activities described below for building ECDs, use information contained within the ELHs and LDS, as illustrated in Figure 8.

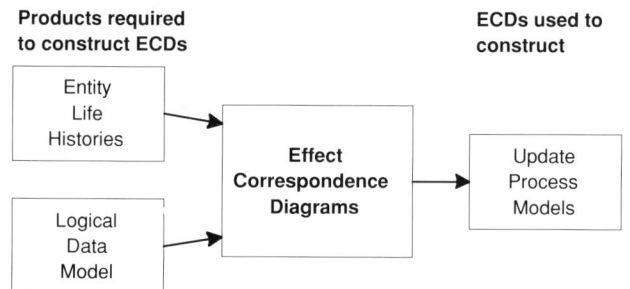

Figure 8: Effect Correspondence Diagrams: Precursor products and dependant products

The step-by-step approach below follows the activities for constructing ECDs described in the SSADM Version 4 Reference Manual.

Activity a – Draw a box representing each entity affected by the event

Automatable? Fully
Products Used: ELHs

Notes Relating To Example
Six boxes are created at this stage – Rental Booking; Customer; Rental Day; Car Day; Branch; Car.

Activity b – Draw separate boxes for simultaneous effects

Automatable? Fully
Products Used: ELHs

Notes Relating To Example
Two effects shown for Branch in Figure 7 are simultaneous effects: Customer Car Return may cause one Branch to gain responsibility for a Car and another Branch to lose responsibility for a Car. Thus two instances of Branch may be affected, Branch [issuing branch] and Branch [receiving branch]. Two instances of Branch are therefore included in the ECD, qualified by the role names.

Supplementary Guidance Notes
It is essential that a CASE tool enables the user to clearly distinguish in the ELHs between simultaneous effects or

'roles' (affecting separate instances of an entity type) and 'optional effects' (mutually exclusive effects on one instance of an entity type). This is done in the ELHs with separate sets of parentheses; round brackets for mutually exclusive effects and square brackets for roles. The order of the parentheses is reversed in the ECD to role name followed by effect name.

The ECD example in the SSADM Version 4 Reference Manual is built from ELHs without parallelism and parallelism is not explicitly dealt with within the ECD activities. An event appearing more than once within the parallel bar notation has multiple simultaneous effects and so is covered by Activity b. Where an event appears once within the parallel bars and once outside the parallel bars, there are optional effects (covered by Activity c).

Activity c – Include optional effects

Automatable? Partially
Products Used: ELHs

Notes Relating To Example
Customer Car Return has two alternative effects on Car (Figure 6) – either it is returned to the same Branch or it is returned to another Branch. In either case it affects the same Car. A selection between the mutually exclusive effects is introduced under the original Car component.

There is still one effect missing. There are three effects of the event on the Branch ELH (shown in Figure 7), including the two roles dealt with in Activity b. The third effect is concerned with the case where the customer returns the car to the issuing branch. Only one instance of Branch is affected in this case.

Supplementary Guidance Notes
Optional effects are all those appearing on an ELH which are not roles, where there are two or more mutually exclusive effects upon a single instance of the entity type. A set of mutually exclusive effects may reflect more than one condition: there may be nested conditions which will need to be distinguished in the eventual UPM. Separate conditions should ideally be distinguished on the ELHs and ECDs within the 'optional effect' parentheses, by the use of commas. It is

unrealistic to expect a CASE tool to recognise the nested conditions within a set of mutually exclusive effects, which is why this activity is classified as only partially automatable.

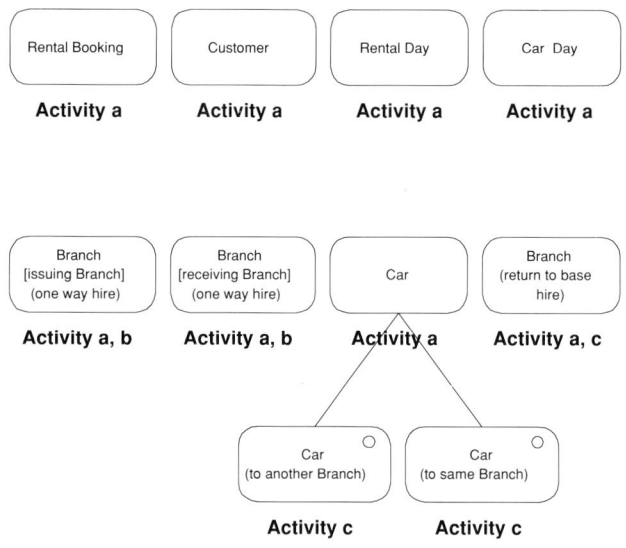

Figure 9: Effect Correspondence Diagram up to Activity c

At the end of Activity c there should be an elementary box for each effect of the event throughout the ELHs. The construction of an ECD for each event on the ELHs is relatively simple and mechanistic but, without CASE tool support, is a time-consuming and error-prone task for the systems analyst.

The ECD based on the EU-Rent ELHs, up to Activity c is as Figure 9.

Activity d – Add iterations to effects

Automatable? Partially
Products Used: ELHs, LDM

Notes Relating To Example
The access point for the event Customer Car Return is Rental Booking (see Figure 1) – it causes the death of a single Rental Booking. Rental Booking is the master of Rental Day which is also an effect on the ECD. The ECD

processes a set of Rental Days owned by the Rental Booking so an iteration of Rental Days is introduced by Activity d on to the ECD (as shown on the completed ECD in Figure 10).

Supplementary Guidance Notes
In order to automate Activity d, an unambiguous access path through the LDS (Figure 1) must be evident. In the above example, Rental Booking, Car and Branch all appear on the ECD. A single Rental Booking is the access point for the event – this must be known for the remaining access path to be determined. So one Rental Booking is accessed, which is owned by one Car which may be swapped from one Branch to another if the Car is returned to a different Branch from where it was issued. There are no iterations in this access path.

The access path may appear to be unambiguous, but it can be seen from Figure 1 that there is an alternative access path from Rental Booking to the issue and return Branches and then on to find a set of Cars for one of the Branches. This would mean an iteration of Cars being introduced during Activity d. The access path is ambiguous and only the analyst (who may need to consult the ELHs) can determine which is correct, which is why this activity is classified as only partially automatable.

Activity e – Add one-to-one correspondences between effects

Automatable? Partially
Products Used: ELHs, LDM

Notes Relating To Example
The access point for the event Customer Car Return is Rental Booking – this information must be supplied by the analyst. From there, the access path may be followed on the LDS (Figure 1). For one Rental Booking read, there will be one Customer, one Car and a set of Rental Days read. For each Rental Day, there will be one Car Day read. Only if the car is returned to a different branch, will Branch [issuing branch] and Branch [receiving branch] be accessed.

Supplementary Guidance Notes
As with Activity d, the access path must be known in order to allocate correspondences. Similar obstacles to

automation therefore exist to those described in the previous activity.

Activity f – Merge iterative effects

Automatable? No
Products Used: Not applicable

Notes Relating To Example
There is no example of optional iterative effects within the Customer Car Return event.

Supplementary Guidance Notes
This activity is concerned with iterations containing selections. Where a master entity has a selection of effects and the same selection appears under an iteration of detail entities, it may be necessary to re-express these as a selection of iterations. Although it may be theoretically possible to automate this procedure, it depends upon very disciplined naming of selections and correct correspondences being correctly established in the previous activity. Furthermore, it is a situation which rarely appears within an ECD and so would provide little productivity gain for the analyst user. For these reasons, it is assumed that this activity is not automatable.

Activity g – Add non-updated entities

Automatable? No
Products Used: LDM

Notes Relating To Example
There are no examples of non-updated entities within the example.

Supplementary Guidance Notes
These are boxes to indicate where entities need to be read but not updated. This may be to traverse the LDS or to provide additional data to produce an output report. This should rarely be required and this activity should not be used as a substitute for rigorous ELH analysis. Since the detailed content of output reports may not have been defined at this point in the analysis, there is a further opportunity to add enquiry only entities during the production of UPMs (Activity e).

Activity h – Add event data	*Automatable?* No
Products Used: Not applicable

Notes Relating To Example
The data required for the Event is Booking #, Customer Return Time.

Supplementary Guidance Notes
Again the CASE tool need only support the analyst user to annotate the diagram with the necessary text.

The completed Customer Car Return ECD is at Figure 10. |
| Conclusion | The first two activities in building an ECD are fully automatable and the third is almost fully automatable. These activities are all based solely on the ELHs; the access path of the ECD, which may be ambiguous and is complex to infer, is not required. The first three activities are recommended to CASE tool suppliers as a start point for automatic generation of ECDs. They are the most easily automated, would significantly increase the productivity of the analyst user and would result in a 'skeleton' ECD, free from transcription errors, for the analyst to build upon. |
| 3.4.4 Generating Update Process Models (UPMs) | The activities described below for building UPMs, use information contained within the ELHs, ECDs and LDM, as illustrated at Figure 11.

The example event, Customer Car Return, from the case study EU-Rent, is now developed to create an Update Process Model (UPM) from the above ECD. The same step-by-step approach is used as in the last section, this time following the activities described in the SSADM Version 4 Reference Manual.

The initial three activities, a (Specify event name), b (Specify event data) and c (Specify Effect Correspondence Diagram), are preliminaries to building the UPM covered in the ECD material, so we begin the detailed explanation from activity d. |

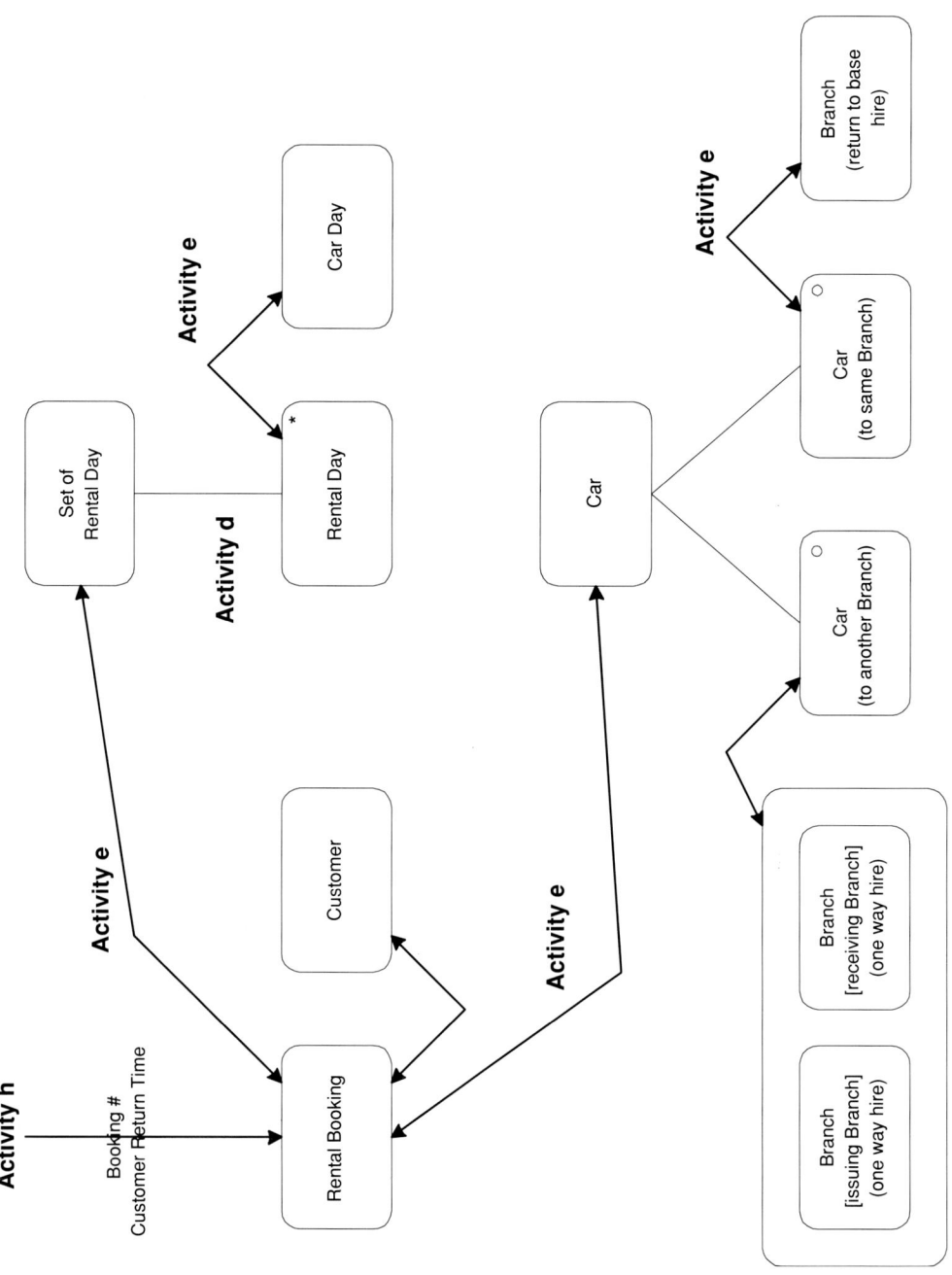

Figure 10: Completed Effect Correspondence Diagram for Customer Car Return

Chapter 3
Case tools and SSADM products

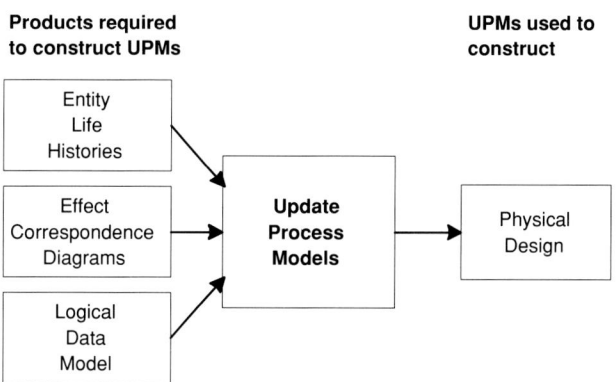

Figure 11: Update Process Models: Precursor products and dependant products

Activity d – Specify Event Output

Automatable? No
Products Used: Not Applicable

Notes Relating To Example
The output required for Customer Car Return is a simple reply code indicating the success or failure of the event.

Supplementary Guidance Notes
Where significant output is required for the event, it should be defined as an output structure as for an Enquiry Process Model (described in section 3.4.6).

Activity e – Extend the ECD with enquiry-only entities

Automatable? No
Products Used: Not Applicable

Notes Relating To Example
There is no output requirement so there are no examples of non-updated entities within the example.

Supplementary Guidance Notes
This is the same as activity g of building ECDs, done here in order to specify the read-only entities required for output. The activity must be carried out by the analyst who needs to be able to amend the ECD.

Automating SSADM Projects

Activity f – Group effects in one-to-one correspondence

Automatable? Fully
Products Used: ECD

Notes Relating To Example
Each correspondence arrow indicates a group of effects. In the example (Figure 12), there are four groups, each of which has been given a name based on a concatenation of the effect names it encompasses. Where a full concatenation of names is excessively long, they have been truncated and suffixed with 'etc' (as in Rental Booking, Customer, Car etc).

Supplementary Guidance Notes
There are two parts to the activity: grouping and naming, and each may be fully automated. It is unnecessary for a CASE tool to produce an amended ECD, but groups must be recognised and named in order to produce the UPM. Recognition of a group is straightforward; it relates directly to one set of correspondence arrows. Naming can be based on a concatenation of the effect names within the correspondence group, truncated and suffixed with 'etc' where necessary. This will normally produce a meaningful name, although naming may be made more reliable by assigning priorities to determine which effect names should be dropped from the group name. In the example below, 'Rental Booking' is maintained within the name because it is the access point to the ECD.

Similarly, 'Car (to another branch)' is kept within the group name rather than 'Branch [issuing]' because it is a conditional effect. Automatically generated group names should be modifiable by the analyst user once the UPM is produced.

Chapter 3
Case tools and SSADM products

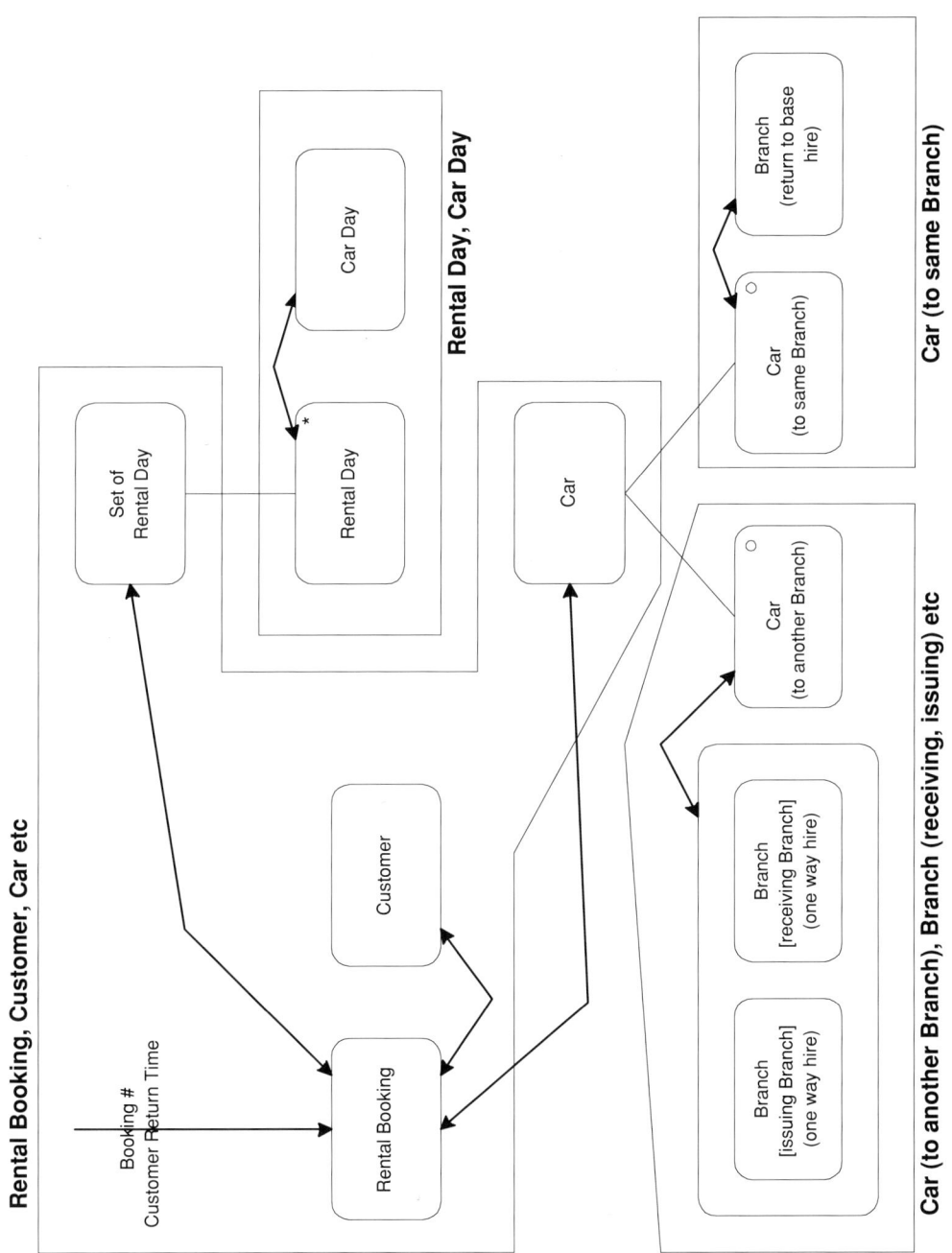

Figure 12: ECD with grouped effects

39

Activity g – List operations

Automatable? Fully
Products Used: ELHs, ECD

Notes Relating To Example
The UPM produced (Figure 13) contains a fairly long list of operations. Note that there are two sets of operations for entity type Branch: one set for the Branch gaining the Car and one set for the Branch losing the Car.

Supplementary Guidance Notes
A full description of the required operations is given under activity g within the SSADM Version 4 Reference Manual and these are not repeated in full here. The UPM operations are either inherited from the ELHs or generated by this activity. The two types are handled quite differently and they are discussed in turn below.

In SSADM, the operations inherited from the ELHs have to be changed to make sense within the context of a UPM. For example, the Car ELH (Figure 6) shows operation 10 as 'Cut from Branch using the responsibility of'. Within a UPM it will no longer be clear that it is a Rental Booking which must be tied to the Branch, and so the operation must be changed to (Figure 13 operation 13): 'Cut Car from Branch using the responsibility of'.

Gain and lose operations are not required within UPMs; these could be dropped automatically by a CASE tool.

Where UPMs are automatically generated by a CASE tool, it is likely to be simpler to encourage the user to reference the entity within the ELH operation so that it may be incorporated within the UPM without amendment. So, in our example, the user will define the ELH operation as 'Cut Car from Branch using the responsibility of'. This approach could be enforced; a CASE tool could control the text within the ELH operation since there are a limited number of predictable formats (listed within the SSADM Version 4 Reference Manual).

As well as incorporating the operations from the ELHs, a CASE tool is able to perfectly generate all the remaining operations that are necessary. Each entity (or role) requires an operation to read or create it, check it is in a valid state (from the ELH valid prior states), set the exit state and write it. All of these operations are straightforward to generate. However, a problem will arise when generating the integrity checks if the state indicators have been allocated manually on the ELHs in such a way that they conflict with the structure of the ELH. Should the CASE tool generate the state indicator checks based on the structure or on the states allocated by the analyst?

Activity h – Convert to Jackson-like notation

Automatable? Fully
Products Used: ECD

Notes Relating To Example
The four groups shown in the amended ECD (Figure 12) convert to four structure boxes in the UPM in Figure 13. A sequence has been assigned to the processing of the separate branches of the structure; processing must begin with the group containing the access point (ie Rental Booking, Customer, Car etc) but the order of processing of the two branches of the structure is unimportant. Note the condition (to same branch)/(to another branch) is preserved within the Jackson structure, as is the iteration of Rental Days.

Supplementary Guidance Notes
This activity is fully automatable although the processing required is fairly complex.

Each correspondence group within the ECD is identified and named as part of activity f. Activity h involves transforming the identified groups into a Jackson structure. The group containing the access point becomes the top structure box of the UPM. Other groups are merged to become either an iterated or selected component of the UPM. The sequence of processing branches within a UPM is generally unimportant.

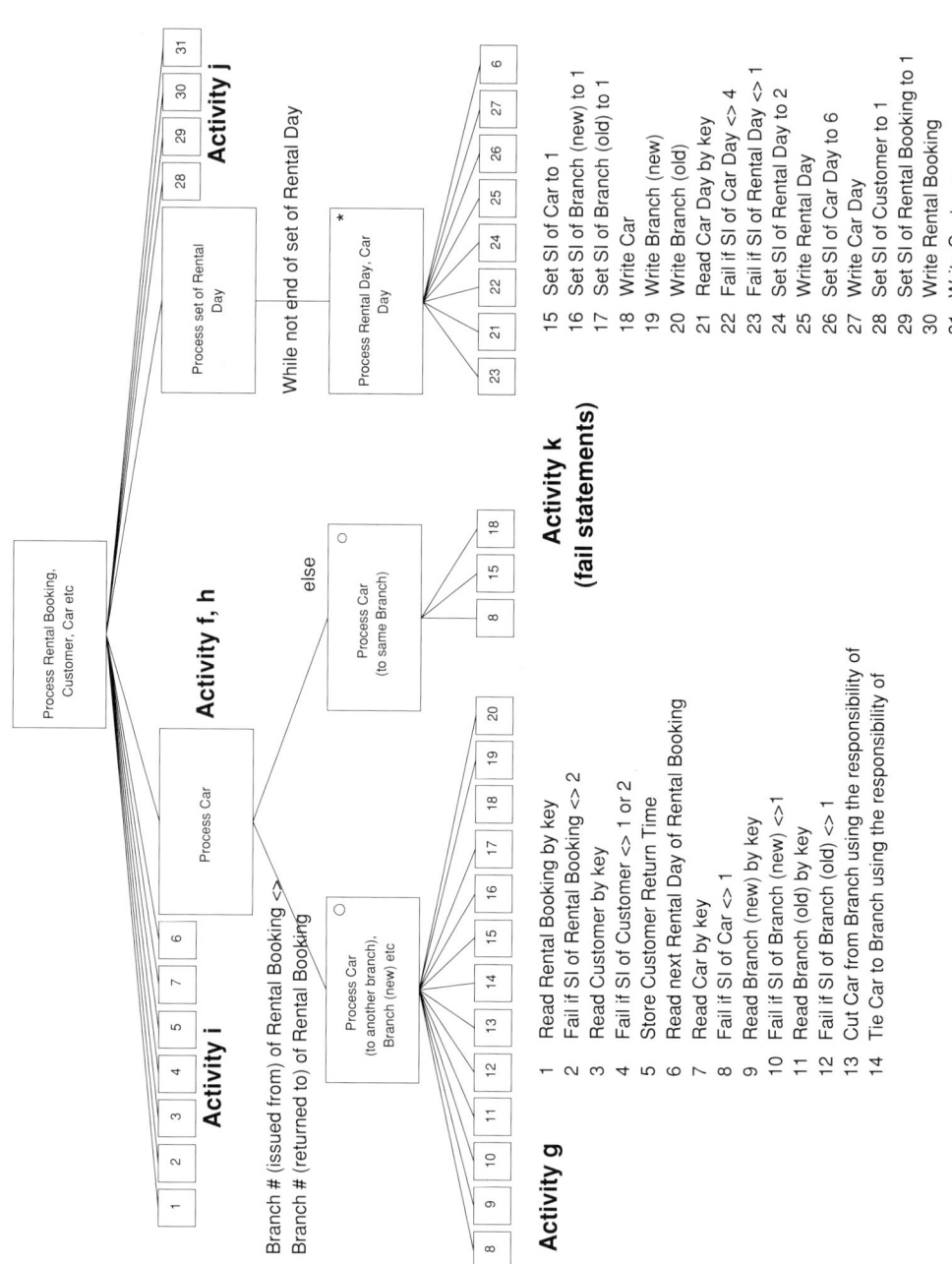

Figure 13: Update Process Model for Customer Car Return

Chapter 3
Case tools and SSADM products

Activity i – Allocate operations to structure

Automatable? Fully
Products Used: ECD

Notes Relating To Example
The operations are allocated (generally once) throughout the structure of the UPM below.

However, note that some structure boxes do not have operations; these are the ones which are introduced to make a valid Jackson structure and are not a direct result of a merged set of corresponding ECD boxes. For example, as shown in Figure 13, the structure box 'Process Car' is introduced as a selection for the condition 'Car (to same branch)/Car (to another branch)'; the entity type Car in the ECD is merged within 'Process Booking, Customer, Car etc'. Similarly, 'Process Set of Rental Days' is introduced as an iteration and so does not 'own' operations.

Supplementary Guidance Notes
Although fully automatable, allocating operations to the UPM structure is fairly complex. Each operation is allocated to the structure box processing that entity, unless an iteration of entity occurrences must be read, where a 'read-ahead' is required prior to the iterated processing. See the read-ahead of Rental Day (in Figure 13) for illustration.

The following need to be allocated, in the following order, for each entity processed: read operations; state indicator checks; create operations (where necessary); operations from the ELHs; operations to set the exit state of the entity; and write operations. The format of each of these operations is shown in the example UPM, except for creates, which should read: 'Create <Entity Name>'.

A CASE tool supplier could choose to optimise state indicator settings, removing the set operation and write operation where the state indicator has not been changed by the event (although this optimisation has not been applied to the UPM example).

43

Activity j – Allocate conditions to structure

Automatable? Partially
Products Used: ELH

Notes Relating To Example
In the example, the 'end of set' condition on 'Process Rental Day, Car Day' could be added automatically. The condition allocated for the 'Process Car' selection in the UPM could not be determined from the ELHs and would be added by the analyst user, following UPM generation.

Supplementary Guidance Notes
'End of set' conditions may always be automatically allocated to iterations. Selections may also often be derivable from the ELHs, since alternative effects are often a result of different prior states. However, as in the example below, some conditions are dependent upon other variables than the state indicator, and so must be added by the analyst user following generation. This activity is therefore not fully automatable.

Note that it is at this stage that the analyst may spot a recognition problem within the UPM. This is where there is insufficient information available to evaluate a selection (or condition on an iteration) because of the order of processing. Recognition problems and their solution using quits and resumes are well-documented within publications concerned with Jackson Structured Programming. The CASE tool is not able to identify recognition problems, but it must allow the analyst user to amend the generated UPM to add quits and resumes (using the same notation as that in ELHs).

Activity k – Specify integrity error conditions

Automatable? No
Products Used: Not applicable

Notes Relating To Example
The only integrity error conditions in the example (in Figure 13) are listed amongst the operations.

Supplementary Guidance Notes
Integrity error conditions are generally interpreted as 'fail' operations using the valid prior states from the ELHs. This activity relates to any remaining conditions

not documented within the ELHs; these must be added by the analyst user.

The final two activities l (Specify error outputs (logical and physical)) and m (Walk through the structure) are not relevant to this discussion. Error outputs, are not usually specified until physical design, and will not appear on the UPM.

To summarise, UPMs may be almost fully generated automatically. The initial activities up to Activity e complete the ECD and do not relate to building a UPM. The remaining activities may all be executed successfully by a CASE tool, except activities j and k. For activity j, it is generally quick and simple for the user to add missing conditions; only recognition problems (which are extremely rare in UPMs) may be more time-consuming. Activity k, specify integrity error conditions, can usually be executed in full by a CASE tool and it is only occasionally that further conditions will need to be added by the user.

It requires little judgement to build a UPM, since almost all the necessary information is already specified within the ECD and ELHs. They are, however, very time-consuming and error-prone if constructed 'manually' by an analyst. They are, therefore, an excellent subject for CASE tool automation.

3.4.5 Generating Enquiry Access Paths (EAPs)

The activities described below for building EAPs, use information contained within the LDM, as illustrated in Figure 14.

The enquiry selected to illustrate Enquiry Access Paths (EAPs) and Enquiry Process Models (EPMs) is named Branch Booking Enquiry. The requirement is to list the cars for which a branch is currently responsible, followed by those cars that it owns but is not currently responsible. For cars for which the branch is responsible, further details are required about current bookings and the renting customer. The layout of the enquiry is illustrated at Figure 15.

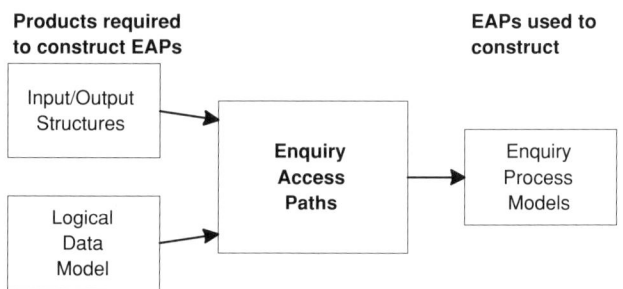

Figure 14: Enquiry Access Paths: Precursor products and dependant products

The attributes within Branch Line (Figure 15) are all within entity type Branch, those within Car Line are within Car, those within Booking Line are within Rental Booking and those within Customer line are within Customer. The LDS is the same as that shown in section 3.4.2.

The activities for constructing Enquiry Access Paths are described in the SSADM Version 4 Reference Manual. As in the previous two sections a step-by-step approach is used to examine the extent to which the production of EAPs may be automated.

Activity a – Informally identify the entities which must be accessed

Automatable? No
Products Used: Input/Output Structures

Notes Relating To Example
The entity types of interest are Branch, Car, Rental Booking and Customer.

Supplementary Guidance Notes
This activity is carried out by the analyst prior to constructing the Required View.

Chapter 3
Case tools and SSADM products

Branch Line	Branch # 999		Name?XXXXXXXXXXXXXXXXXXXXXX			
Car Line	Car Reg No	XXXXXXX	Owner?	Y/N	Responsible?	Y/N
Booking Line	dd/mm/yy to dd/mm/yy		Return Branch # 999			
Customer Line	Licence No XXXXXXXXXX		Name XXXXXXXXXXXXXXXXX			
Booking Line	dd/mm/yy to dd/mm/yy		Return Branch # 999			
Customer Line	Licence No XXXXXXXXXX		Name XXXXXXXXXXXXXXXXX			
Car Line	Car Reg No	XXXXXXX	Owner?	Y/N	Responsible?	Y/N
Booking Line	dd/mm/yy to dd/mm/yy		Return Branch # 999			
Customer Line	Licence No XXXXXXXXXX		Name XXXXXXXXXXXXXXXXX			
Car Line	Car Reg No	XXXXXXX	Owner?	Y/N	Responsible?	Y/N
Car Line	Car Reg No	XXXXXXX	Owner?	Y/N	Responsible?	Y/N

Figure 15: Output layout for Branch Booking Enquiry

Activity b – Draw the Required View

Automatable? No
Products Used: Logical Data Model

Notes Relating To Example
The Required View is shown in Figure 16 is a subset of the LDS. Note that both relationships between Branch and Car are needed.

Supplementary Guidance Notes
This Required View (Figure 16) needs to be specified by the analyst user. The CASE tool needs to support the view definition but has no basis on which to deduce it.

Activity c – Redraw the Required View as an entity (Jackson) structure

Automatable? Partially
Products Used: Required View

Notes Relating To Example
The EAP created (Figure 17) shows that the processing for one of the sets of cars for a branch must be completed before the other set of cars is processed. However, despite the directional correspondences, it does not show which set must be processed first. The

selection of Rental Booking (current)/Rental Booking (not current) is required because only details of current bookings and their customers are needed. The selection of Car (owned, responsible)/Car (owned, not responsible) is needed to avoid listing twice that set of cars for which the branch is both responsible and owner.

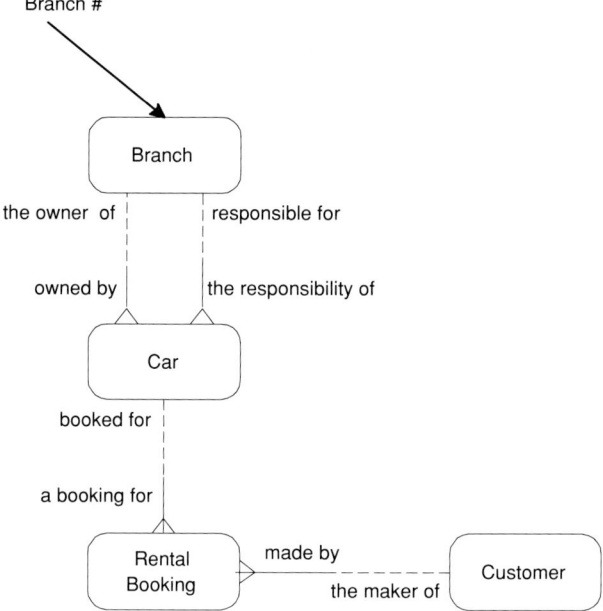

Figure 16: Required View for Branch Booking Enquiry

Supplementary Guidance Notes
This activity involves building the Enquiry Access Path (activity d merely adds the data required for access). In many cases there is a clear and unambiguous access path, and the EAP may be successfully and completely built by a CASE tool.

Many of the same arguments apply here as those described earlier in activities d, e, f of generating Effect Correspondence Diagrams since EAPs and ECDs express the same information using the same notation (except that EAPs use directional correspondences).

Iterations may be identified by examining the cardinality of the relationships on the Required View. One-to-one correspondences exist between entity types where the direction of access is 'up' the relationship, and between an entity type and a set of details when the direction of access is 'down' the relationship. This can normally be deduced from the Required View by the CASE tool, unless the access path is ambiguous, as it is between Branch and Car in the example. It is not clear from the Required View alone, that both sets of cars ('owned' and 'responsible for') must be read, one set after another. It is equally reasonable that after each owned car, the responsible Branch should be accessed and this would require a different EAP. Where there is more than one possible access path, the analyst user may need to amend the generated EAP.

Selections must also be added by the analyst user since it is impossible to tell which, if any, are needed.

Activity d – List the key or non-key attributes used for entry

Automatable? No
Products Used: Required View

Notes Relating To Example
Branch # is the key attribute required for access in this example.

Supplementary Guidance Notes
Where the enquiry trigger is a simple list, it is inherited directly from the Required View and documented on the EAP. If the structure of the data contains iterations or selections, it should be documented separately by the analyst user as a Jackson structure. The completed EAP is at Figure 17.

To summarise, EAPs may be partially generated by a CASE tool, but the potential productivity gains are lower than from the generation of ECDs and UPMs. Complex enquiries are likely to require significant intervention by the analyst user. The process has strong parallels with the construction of ECDs, but in the case of EAPs the Required View must be analyst-built whereas the ECD 'skeleton' may be generated automatically from the ELHs, saving the analyst a significant amount of time and avoiding inevitable transcription errors.

Automating SSADM Projects

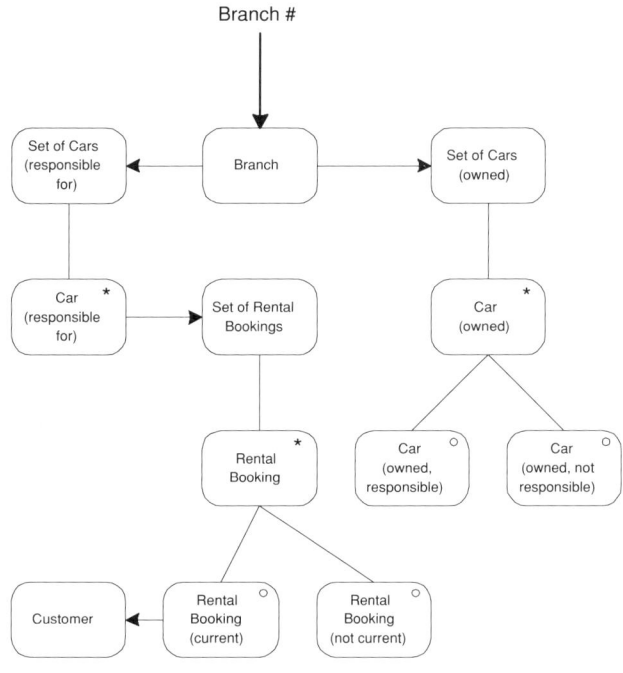

Figure 17: Enquiry Access Path for Branch Booking Enquiry

3.4.6 Generating Enquiry Process Models (EPMs)

The activities described below for building EPMs, use information contained within the Enquiry Access Paths and Input/Output Structures, as illustrated at Figure 18.

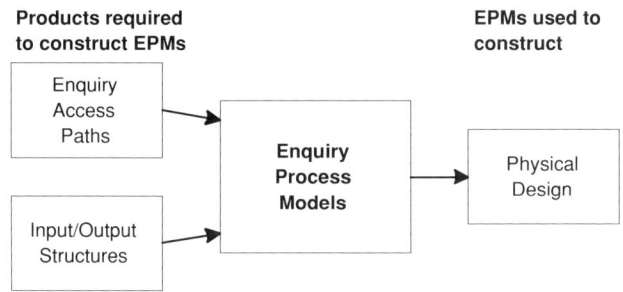

Figure 18: Enquiry Process Models: Precursor products and dependant products

Chapter 3
Case tools and SSADM products

The same enquiry example, Branch Booking Enquiry, is now used to illustrate Enquiry Process Models (EPMs), built from the EAP constructed in the previous section and shown in Figure 17.

The activities for constructing EPMs are described in the SSADM Version 4 Reference Manual. As in the previous sections a step-by-step approach is used, this time examining the extent to which the production of EPMs may be automated.

The initial three activities, a (Specify enquiry name), b (Specify enquiry trigger) and c (Specify enquiry access path), are preliminaries to building the EPM, already covered in section 3.4.5, so we begin our detailed explanation from activity d.

Activity d – Specify enquiry

Automatable? No
Products Used: Input/Output Structures

Notes Relating To Example
The enquiry output, expressed as a Jackson structure, is at Figure 19.

Supplementary Guidance Notes
The definition of an output data structure can be supported but not generated by a CASE tool.

Activity e – Group accesses on the Enquiry Access Path

Automatable? Fully
Products Used: EAP

Notes Relating To Example
The correspondence has already been identified on the EAP produced in section 3.4.5, Figure 17 (Activity c).

Supplementary Guidance Notes
This activity is likely to be unnecessary with a CASE tool. Since the correspondences have been identified on the EAP, this can be converted to an input data structure in the Jackson style (Activity f) without further analyst intervention. This assumes of course that any access path ambiguities have been resolved on the EAP.

Automating SSADM Projects

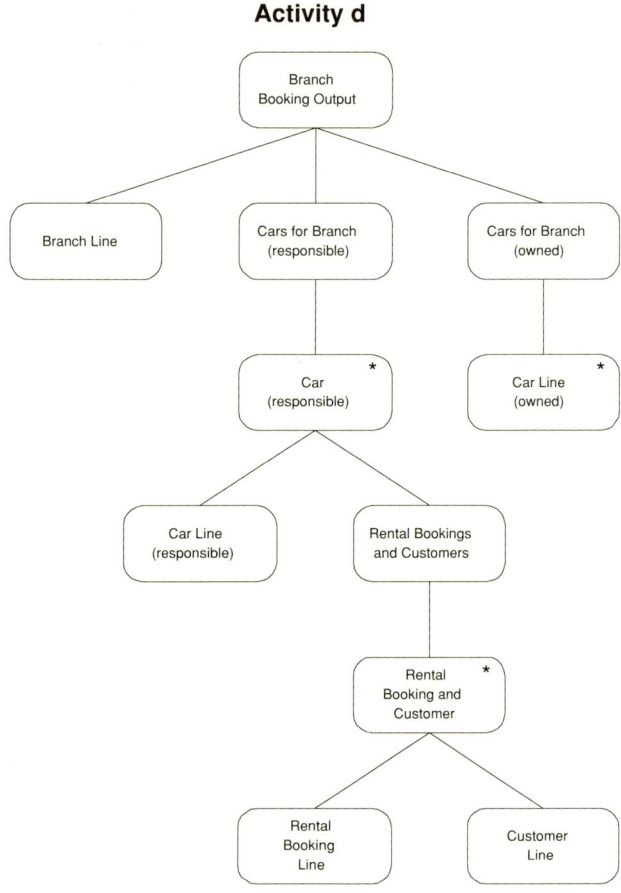

Figure 19: Output data structure for Branch Booking Enquiry

Activity f – Convert to Jackson-like notation

Automatable? Fully
Products Used: EAP

Notes Relating To Example
The three correspondence groups shown in the amended EAP convert to three structure boxes. The new structure is shown on the left hand side of Figure 20.

Chapter 3
Case tools and SSADM products

Activity g – Identify correspondences between input and output data structures

Automatable? No
Products Used: Input and output data structures

Notes Relating To Example
Correspondences are shown by the double-headed arrows in the diagram below.

Supplementary Guidance Notes
Correspondences must be specified by the analyst user. However, validation by the CASE tool is required to ensure that the resulting correspondences may be successfully merged in activity h. Structure clashes found during this activity need to be resolved by the user before proceeding to activity h.

Activity h – Merge the input and output data structures.

Automatable? Fully
Products Used: Input and output data structures

Notes Relating To Example
The completed EPM (Figure 21) shows that the structure resulting from this activity has three sequential parts to the top-level sequence. Unlike UPMs, the order of processing branches here is important as it determines the order of data output. In the diagram above showing the input and output data structures, Cars (owned) are processed after Cars (responsible for) and it is important that this order is maintained within the final EPM.

Supplementary Guidance Notes
Components of the input and output data structures in one-to-one correspondence are merged in the same way as when converting to Jackson structures (see the notes for activity h of section 3.4.4).

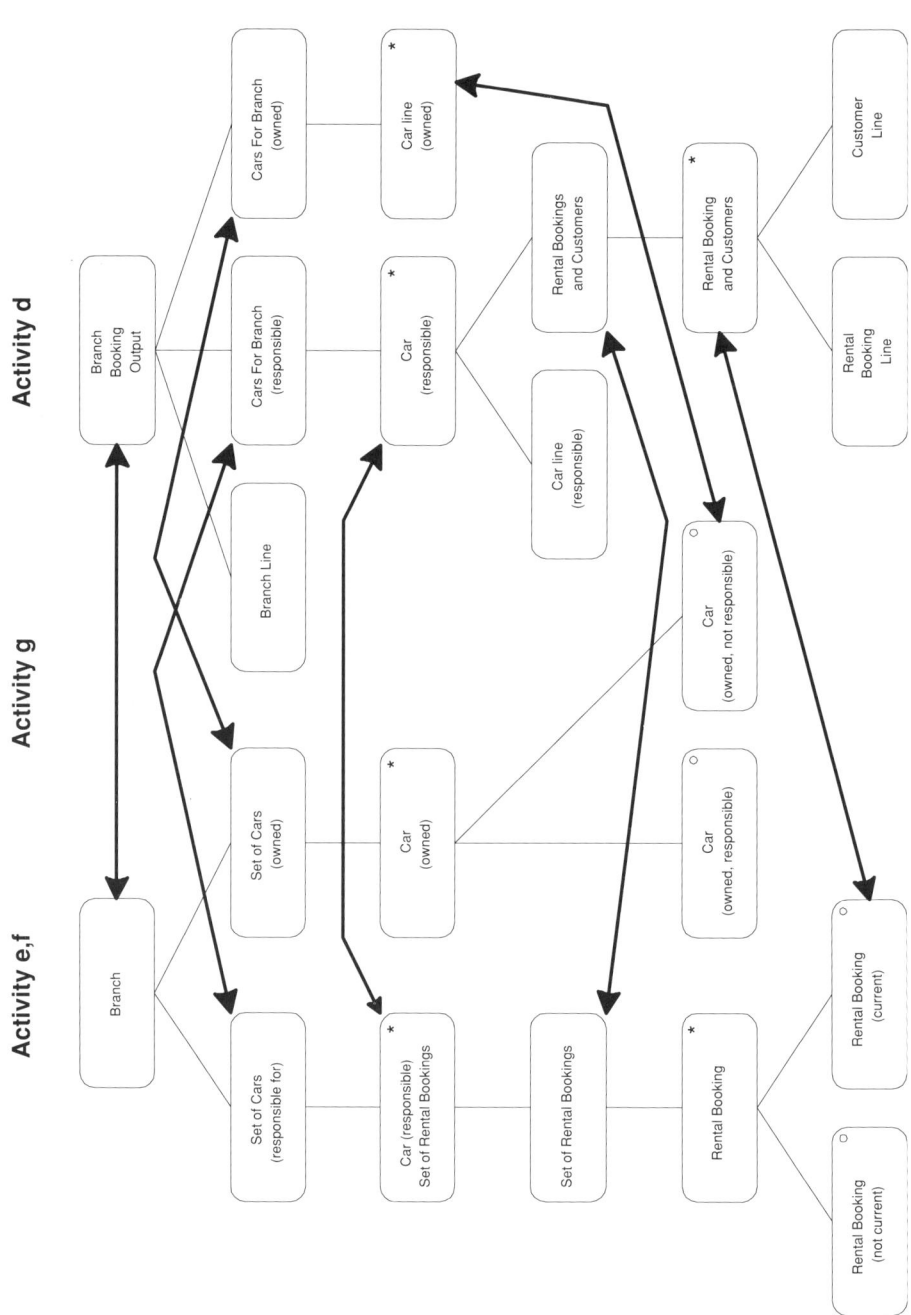

Figure 20: Input and output structures with correspondences

Activity i – List the operations and allocate them to the structure	*Automatable?* Fully *Products Used*: Merged process structure **Notes Relating To Example** In the completed EPM (Figure 21) the read operations have been allocated to the structure. The EAP makes it clear which entities must be read: a Branch; a set of Cars (responsible for); a set of Rental Bookings; a Customer; a set of Cars (owned). The entry point and key(s) to be used are also shown. However, in order that operations syntax is generated correctly, where there is more than one relationship between accessed entity types, the relationship names used to qualify the read must match that on the LDS. So 'responsible for', which qualifies the set of Cars read, must match the required relationship name between Branch and Car on the LDS. **Supplementary Guidance Notes** It is only possible to fully automate this activity if the access path is unambiguous (see section 3.4.5, activity c). In particular the EAP will need to identify the data items and relationships used to identify the entities accessed if the correct read statements are to be generated. The alternative approach is to use the CASE tool to generate a processing structure, and for the analyst to add the read operations manually at this point.
Activity j – Allocate conditions to structure	*Automatable?* Partially *Products Used:* Merged process structure **Notes Relating To Example** 'End of set' conditions may be automatically allocated to the three iterations within the EPM below. The two selections shown are both dependent upon attributes and must be added by the analyst user, following EPM generation.

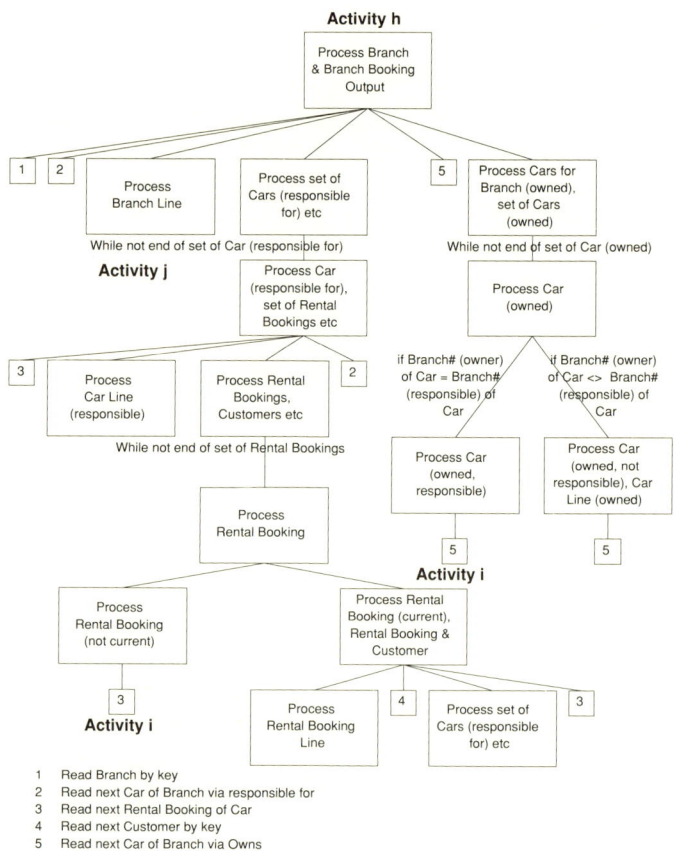

Figure 21: Enquiry Process Model for Branch Booking Enquiry

Supplementary Guidance Notes

'End of set' conditions may be automatically allocated to iterations. Selections, however, must be added by the analyst, so this activity is only partially automatable.

The notes for activity j of section 3.4.5 regarding recognition problems apply equally here.

Activity k – Specify integrity error conditions

Automatable? Partially
Products Used: ELHs

Notes Relating To Example
Integrity error conditions have not been shown in this example.

Supplementary Guidance Notes
An enquiry process is specified assuming a valid database, so 'fail' operations, which check that the entity is in a valid state to receive the enquiry, may be added by the user following the read operations. The allocation of these could be automated if enquiries were included in the ELHs, or there was some other means of specifying that the enquiry is legitimate only for certain ranges of state indicator (eg exclude cars with a state indicating the car had been written-off).

The two last activities, l (Specify error outputs (logical and physical)) and m (Walk through the structure), are not relevant to this discussion. Error outputs are not usually specified until physical design, and will not appear on the EPM.

To conclude, the production of EPMs is a comparable process to the production of UPMs. However, EPMs are less automatable and require more analyst intervention. Furthermore, many enquiries will not need to be specified as EPMs, so the productivity benefits from automation are consequently diminished. EPM generation is therefore a less valuable CASE tool facility than UPM generation.

However, since much of the construction process is common to both EPMs and UPMs, EPM generation could be added as a facility with relatively little extra effort.

3.5 Conclusions

The preceding discussion seeks to illustrate the potential for automating the production of ECDs, UPMs, EAPs and EPMs by CASE tools. ECDs and UPMs are particularly suitable: they are time-consuming for the analyst to produce and much of the process may be automated. EPMs require more analyst intervention in the production process than UPMs; but because the two process modelling techniques are so similar, EPMs could be added to the CASE tool 'menu' once UPM processing has been developed, for little relatively additional effort.

UPMs and EPMs may also be translated mechanically into procedural code (eg COBOL Procedure Division) and into other forms of specification, if required, including:

- Pseudo-code

- Schematic logic (JSP-style Pseudo-code)

- Action Diagrams (Information Engineering Pseudo-code)

- State-transition Diagrams (Information Engineering)

- Fence diagrams (Information Engineering).

In general, it is relatively simple to translate SSADM process models into process specifications from other methodologies or into real code, as long as the target language is procedural and the logic is expressed in terms of sequence, selection and iteration.

Figures 22 and 23 show the EPM (Figure 21) developed in section 3.4.6 as generated in the form of an Action Diagram and as schematic logic.

Given the potential productivity gains to be obtained from the ability to generate ECDs, UPMs, EAPs and EPMs and to translate UPMs and EPMs into other forms of specification, these facilities offer users substantial benefits. CASE tool vendors offering such benefits are also likely to benefit through increased sales potential to new customers and through increased customer satisfaction amongst existing users.

Chapter 3
Case tools and SSADM products

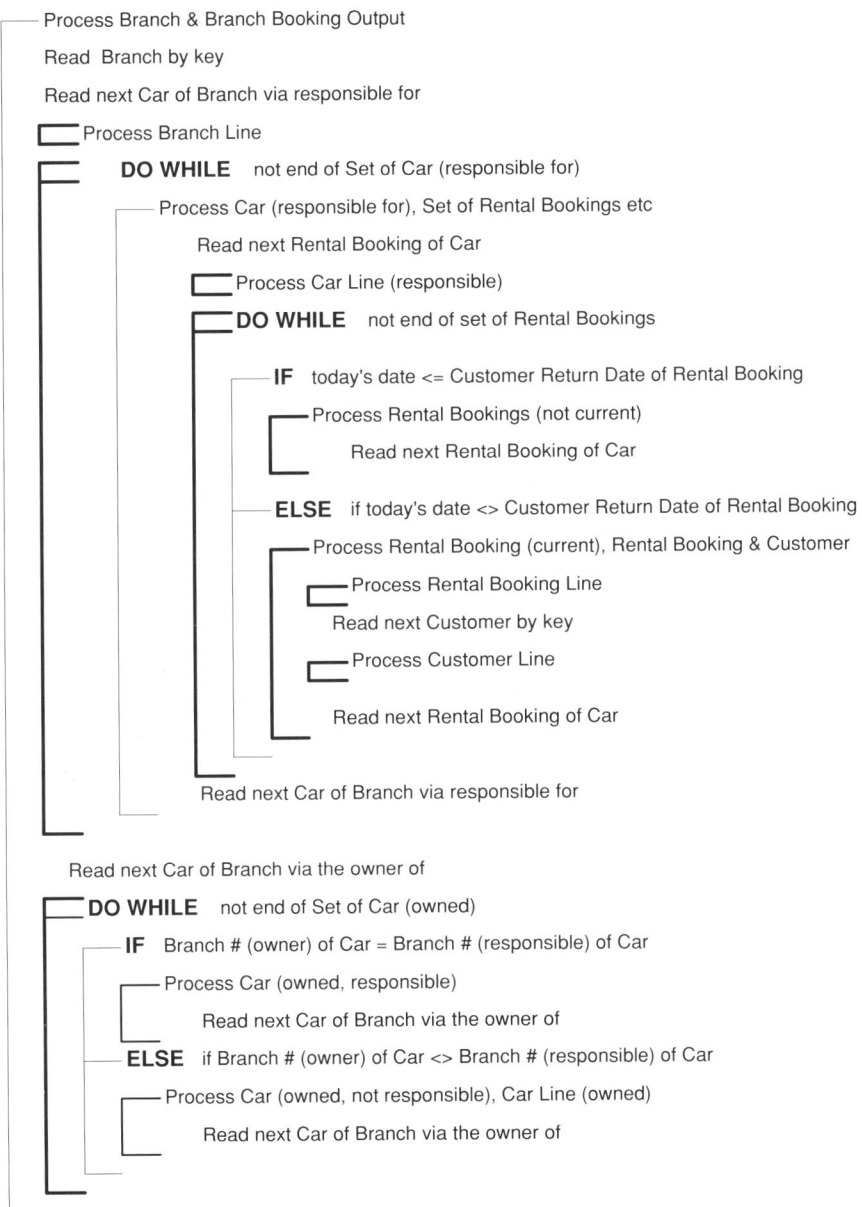

Figure 22: EPM (Figure 21) in the form of an Action Diagram

Branch Booking Enquiry
Process Branch & Booking Output **SEQ**
    Read Branch by key
    Read next Car of Branch via responsible for
    Process Branch Line **SEQ**
    Process Branch Line **END**
    Process Set of Cars (responsible for) etc **ITER WHILE** not end of set of Car (responsible for)
        Process (responsible for), Set of Rental Bookings etc **SEQ**
        Read next Rental Booking of Car
        Process Car Line (responsible) **SEQ**
        Process Car Line (responsible) **END**
        Process Rental Bookings, Customer etc **ITER WHILE** not end of set of Rental Bookings
            Process Rental Booking **SELECT** if today's date > Customer Return Date of Rental Booking
            Process Rental Booking (not current) **SEQ**
                Read next Rental Booking of Car
            Process Rental Booking (not current) **END**
        Process Rental Booking **OR** if today's date <= Customer Return Date of Rental Booking
            Process Rental Booking (current), Rental Booking & Customer **SEQ**
                Process Rental Booking Line **SEQ**
                Process Rental Booking Line **END**
                Read next Customer by key
                Process Customer Line **SEQ**
                Process Customer Line **END**
                Read next Rental Booking of Car
            Process Rental Booking (current), Rental Booking & Customer **END**
        Process Rental Booking **END**
        Process Rental Bookings, Customers etc **END**
        Read next Car of Branch via responsible for
        Process Car (responsible for), Set of Rental Bookings etc **END**
    Process Set of Cars (responsible for) etc **END**
    Read next Car of Branch via the owner of
    Process Cars For Branch (owned), Set of Cars (owned) **ITER WHILE** not end of set of Car (owned)
        Process Car (owned)   **SELECT** if Branch # (owner) of Car = Branch # (responsible) of Car
            Process Car (owned, responsible) **SEQ**
                Read next Car of Branch via the owner of
            Process Car (owned, responsible) **END**
        Process Car (owned) **OR** if Branch # (owner) of Car <> Branch # (responsible) of Car
            Process Car (owned, not responsible), Car Line owned **SEQ**
                Read next Car of Branch via the owner of
            Process Car (owned, not responsible), Car Line owned **END**
        Process Car (owned) **END**
    Process Cars for Branch (owned), Set Of Cars (owned) **END**
Process Branch & Branch Booking Output **END**

Figure 23: EPM (Figure 21) in the form of schematic logic

4 Application generators and SSADM design

4.1 Introduction

There is a widespread but erroneous belief that the later stages of SSADM are somehow irrelevant unless a third-generation language is to be used, and particularly so if an application generator based on an RDBMS is to be used. This belief is based on the misconception that SSADM takes a single development view, applicable to all projects. Although SSADM provides a default process model, it acknowledges that this needs to be modified as a result of factors such as:

- characteristics of the system to be developed

- implementation environment

- type of development

- system cost – either relative to system benefits, or the cost of system failure.

This chapter discusses implementation environment issues that affect the SSADM process model when an application generator is to be used. Its purpose is to give application generator suppliers an understanding of how the latter stages of SSADM can be modified, to assist suppliers in developing more prescriptive product-specific guidance.

SSADM with application generators

SSADM is designed for use with a range of implementation environments. The benefits of application generators are recognised within the method, and their use is encouraged.

Stage 6 (Physical Design) of SSADM assumes that the physical process specifications – the discussion here concentrates on the process design elements – are produced in a form, and to a level of detail, sufficient for direct implementation in a physical environment. This implementation may be via an application generator, a procedural language or a combination of the two. The method recommends that, whenever possible, processing is specified non-procedurally. The form of specification is described in the Physical Design Strategy, and is specific to the implementation environment.

However, SSADM necessarily provides a general approach to physical design, aimed at a range of implementation environments rather than a specific one. Procedures are therefore included for all activities that may be necessary, assuming a 'worst-case' environment of no implementation support tools other than a database management system and a third-generation language compiler. Except for the extreme case, it is not intended that these activities should be carried out as specified. They merely provide an initial template which is tailored to fit the chosen physical environment.

It is not just the physical design procedures that are affected by the use of an application generator. Application generators offer productivity improvements by the use of stereotype system components. The rigorous application of the detailed logical design techniques in SSADM will result in a unique system design for the application, that cannot make use of these stereotype components during implementation. Implementing the unique design will be more costly and take longer than a design based on standard components. The unique design will also implement more of the business rules, and be easier to use. If stereotype components are to be used it is likely that the logical design techniques will need to be modified, or replaced by product-specific alternatives, so that the design produced is capable of taking advantage of the application generator stereotypes.

One of the reasons why the use of SSADM and an application generator have been regarded by some as alternatives rather than complementary approaches, is that application generators are often associated with 'rapid development' methods based on evolutionary prototyping. Alternative development lifecycles, including evolutionary development, are discussed in the ISE Library Volume: *Accelerated SSADM*. This chapter views application generators as a means of speeding-up the implementation of a system specified using SSADM techniques in a conventional lifecycle.

SSADM is not a prescriptive method with a single development thread. It is a flexible method that is capable of being modified to suit project circumstances,

Chapter 4
Application generators and SSADM design

including the use of an application generator. In fact it is the use of SSADM with an application generator that is regarded as the norm, not the (increasingly rare) use of the unamended default model.

Key questions about using application generators

There are four key questions that SSADM practitioners need to have answered if they are to understand how to effectively transform SSADM products into code using a particular application generator:

- what are the design stereotypes used by the application generator?

- at which point(s) within the SSADM Structural Model is it beneficial to replace SSADM activities and products with application generator specific activities and products?

- what are the characteristics of a function that determine whether it should be coded?

    - entirely non-procedurally using the application generator facilities
    - procedurally using a third-generation language
    - using a mix of procedural and non-procedural.

- how are the business rules contained in the Conceptual Model maintained in the implemented system?

In the remainder of this chapter these four key questions are explored in more detail, with the last two being looked at in the context of an example of an SQL implementation of UPMs and EPMs. The chapter concludes with a brief description of the elements that a supplier interface guide should contain. But first, one of the key principles underlying SSADM is briefly discussed.

4.2 The 3-schema specification architecture

The 3-schema specification architecture expresses a key characteristic of an SSADM specification for an IT system – a 'separation of concerns' between the essential business rules and knowledge the system contains; the mechanisms by which the users access the system; and how the logical data model is mapped on to an implementation technology. SSADM adopts the widely accepted philosophy that an 'implementation-independent' system specification is desirable. The expectation is that implementation-independent specifications will outlive their product-specific counterparts, and there will be greater scope for reuse, because they are not constrained by any specific database or processing management system. However, aspects of the system are clearly implementation-specific (eg the specification of the Process Data Interface) in almost all circumstances. The mapping of SSADM products onto the 3-schema specification architecture (Annex A) makes clear which aspects of the system will be implementation-independent and which implementation-specific. The 3-schema specification architecture is an important concept which interface developers need to understand.

The 3-schema specification architecture partitions the system specification into three, as indicated above: the Conceptual Model, the External Design and the Internal Design. These are explained in more detail below and in annex A (for a full discussion see the ISE Library volume: *Customising SSADM* – contact CCTA for more details). This architecture is not merely a top-down decomposition of the system specification. It also represents a separation of software components that should be maintained in the implemented system.

Conceptual Model	The Conceptual Model is the prime concern of an implementation-independent specification. It captures the essential business rules and knowledge that must be transferred between system implementations. Since the Conceptual Model can be implemented using different External Designs and Internal Designs, it must be portable between environments.
External Design	The External Design is much less concerned with implementation-independence than the Conceptual Model. The design of the user interface uses facilities available in the system software (eg the availability of the 'windows' style interface). The value of a logical specification of dialogues, screens and reports is therefore limited. This is already recognised in SSADM. The design of screens and reports is deliberately

postponed until Stage 6 (Physical Design) and the design of 'logical dialogues' is limited to the definition of user roles and the grouping of data items crossing the system boundary. The replacement of the techniques used in SSADM to develop an External Design with a product-specific approach to the definition of the user interface is expected and encouraged. Thus, for example, the use of a GUI can easily be incorporated into SSADM with minimal impact on the Structural Model.

Internal Design

The components of the Internal Design do not appear in an implementation-independent specification. They are concerned with performance of the system using a specific database management system and are not reusable elsewhere The Internal Design procedures in SSADM are based on some universal principles of database design, but are intended to be displaced by product-specific procedures.

Implementation for application generator users

The use of an application generator encourages the adoption of product-specific methods earlier in the system development lifecycle, including those aspects of the system that can be defined in an implementation-independent manner. It is also expected that the SSADM techniques that develop the External and Internal Designs will be replaced by tool-based techniques. However, it is fundamental to the SSADM philosophy that the Conceptual Model should be preserved in the implementation. Therefore, a separation of software components into the Conceptual Model and the Internal and External Designs must be maintained in the application generator code and the application generator must be capable of implementing all the business knowledge contained in the Logical Data Model and entity event models.

4.3 Stereotype systems

When Jackson first published his program design method in 1975: *Principles of Program Design* it was immediately attractive to those who had been looking for a program design methodology. It was convincingly successful in the design of simple programs. The limitations of the method were only revealed when applied to a large and complex program (as one may view a system).

The reverse is true of SSADM. It provides a theory for the design of large and complex information systems. One of the difficulties in selling SSADM is that many people have simpler stereotypes for system design, which work adequately for simple systems, with few users. (The use of different strategies to speed up system development is described in the ISE Library volume: *Accelerated SSADM*)

Stereotypes for how a system and its user interface may be implemented have been successfully embodied in many application generators, including:

- the entity data model is implemented as a relational database

- each entity instance can be displayed as an 'entity reference window'

- each entity type can be displayed as an 'entity list' of entity instances

- updating data is done by over-typing the data displayed in an entity window or list

- most external errors can be specified declaratively using data types and domains

- most integrity errors can be specified using relational integrity rules.

There is no doubt that the use of such stereotypes can greatly speed up the implementation of a system, and the use of SSADM does not preclude their use. In general the better the design fits the stereotypes, the quicker the system can be developed. For the most simple record-keeping systems it may be possible to constrain the design to use only the stereotype components. This approach is similar to some rapid development methods that rely on the use of prototyping tools to define the processing.

Whilst rapid development and prototyping approaches are valuable for certain classes of system, producing the most user-friendly interface, the default approach in

Chapter 4
Application generators and SSADM design

SSADM is to develop a full system meeting 100% of the system requirements. An implementation-independent specification is an essential element of the process. Nevertheless the stereotype systems developed quickly using an application generator can provide a platform for further development and refinement towards the complete system as shown in Figure 24. Not all the functions will require further refinement, as even in complex systems there is usually a significant proportion of functions, such as simple reporting or static data maintenance, which do not have specific customisation requirements.

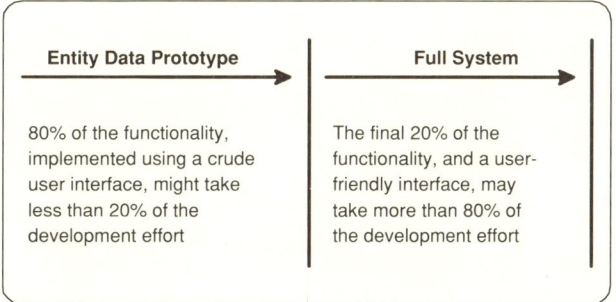

Figure 24: An 80/20 rule

In using application generator stereotypes within an SSADM design it may be necessary to turn off the automated functionality provided by the application generator. In particular, it is likely that SSADM designers will need to turn off the 'binding' of data entry screens to database records, and automatic referential integrity checking.

It is essential that system designers understand the limits of the application generator, so that correct decisions can be made about which stereotypes to use, and which to replace with a more sophisticated alternative. Effective use of SSADM with an application generator is about empowering the designer to make informed decisions about implementation methods. The use of products with simple stereotypes may restrict the ability to implement the design that satisfies all the business requirements. For example, complex business rules about the way entities are deleted may be limited by the application generator to three types of inherited death – RESTRICT, SET NULL and DELETE, in contrast to SSADM which identifies six stereotype design components dealing with deletion of entities. After working with one implementation environment it is easy for designers to fall into the trap of thinking that the tool defines the best or only way to do things.

4.4 Cut-over to application generator products

In section 3.2 the SSADM activities were characterised as product transformations involving discovery, decision making and re-expression. Full automation is only possible for those that involve re-expression alone. This has implications for application generators as well as for CASE tools.

Since there exist in SSADM, transformations that merely re-express a specification in another style without exacting its scope or level of detail, then there is scope for optimising the products (and therefore the activities) in particular circumstances.

4.4.1 SSADM ambition

As has been previously stated, SSADM provides a full set of techniques and procedures for the projects that are implementing the system using a native DBMS and a third-generation programming language. This may be regarded as the 'worst-case' scenario in that it requires a completion of every Step in SSADM up to the end of Stage 6 (Physical Design). The ideal (but not currently achievable) situation is where the system can be specified using the Requirements Specification products, and Stages 5 – 6 of SSADM omitted. This is because almost all the activities involving discovery are completed before the end of Stage 3 (Definition of Requirements). Stage 5, despite being called Logical Design, is mainly concerned with transformation with only a small amount of design. Stage 6 (Physical Design) is largely design activities, but for a specific environment.

Current application generator tools are not sufficiently developed to be able to understand SSADM Stage 3 products directly, and therefore for the majority of projects the 'implementation point' for the system is between the beginning of Stage 5 and end of Stage 6. The implementation point is the point at which the form

Chapter 4
Application generators and SSADM design

and level of detail of the specification is sufficient for the specification to be understood directly (by the programmer or the application generator) without further design or transformation. For a third-generation language the implementation point will be after the production of a program specification and design at a level of detail that can be directly coded in an implementation language such as COBOL. For an application generator the implementation point will be after the completion of the dictionary entries that are required to generate the application, which will typically be less detailed than traditional program specifications.

An environment without any development tools (data dictionary, screen generator, report generator, etc) is likely to require SSADM specifications at the level of detail provided by Stage 6 (Physical Design). A sophisticated application generator enables the cut-over from SSADM specifications to implementation code earlier in the lifecycle. This discussion is summarised diagrammatically in Figure 25.

SSADM has been criticised for requiring the production of UPMs and EPMs which are an 'over-specification' of the event and enquiry processing for application generator environments. Over-specification in this context is usually characterised as the production of excessively detailed procedural specifications, which are difficult to implement (in the manner defined) non-procedurally. This criticism is unfair on two counts. Firstly SSADM does not require the production of UPMs and EPMs. Being part of the default process model does not make a product mandatory. Secondly it is not solely the level of detail that makes them difficult to implement with some application generators. The real difficulty is that SSADM designs database processing around events, whilst some application generators expect processing to be defined non-procedurally around entities. What is loosely termed over-specification is therefore not necessarily a problem of style (procedural versus non-procedural) or level of detail. It is the use of different processing stereotypes (section 4.3) that inhibit an easy translation between SSADM and application generators. Whilst simple systems may be constrained to use only the available stereotypes, the stereotypes may be too

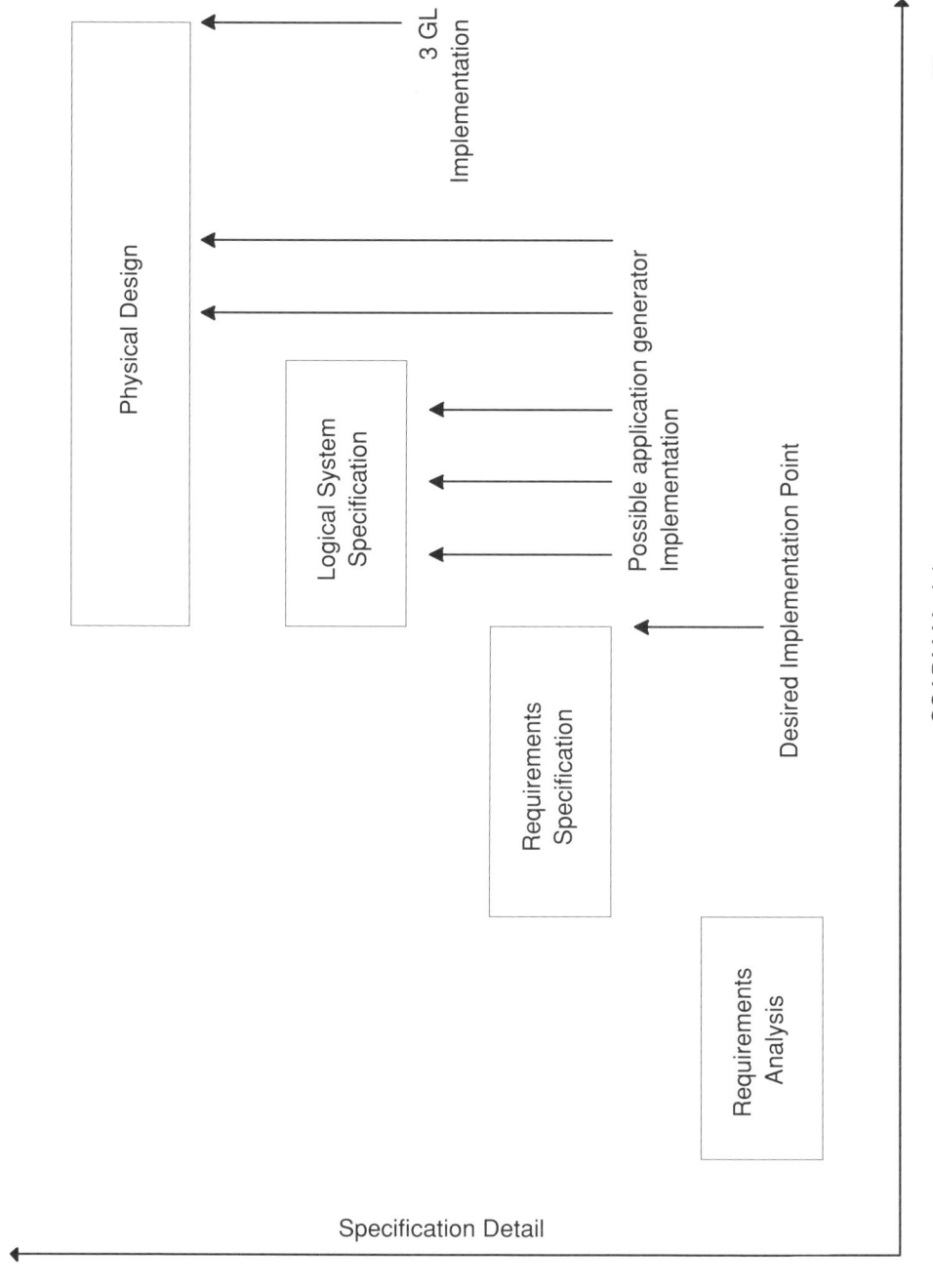

Figure 25: Implementation points in SSADM

general for the more complex, highly customised, systems that can be designed using SSADM.

Some vendors have argued that because their application generators are available on a wide range of hardware platforms, a system design for their product can be considered to be a logical design as well as a physical design. This view is wrong. The term logical design in SSADM does not mean free from all physical constraints. A logical design is a specification that is independent of any particular implementation environment. The correctness of this view was originally recognised as a result of the bitter experience of organisations who had locked themselves into one database management system, transaction manager or other system software. The rapid advance of software development products such as GUIs and object-oriented database management systems has only re-enforced the view that it is system software independence that is the important feature. It is for this reason that the term 'implementation-independent' has been used in this chapter.

One of the key questions for application generator vendors to answer in their interface guides (equivalent to the second of the four defined at the start of this chapter) is how much specification detail is necessary in addition to the Stage 3 products and what form should the specification take. There must still be an implementation-independent specification, but without producing the over-specification described above. Since the Stage 6 products are by definition product-specific, it is only the Stage 5 products that are in question:

- Dialogue Structures (plus Command Structures, Menu Structures, etc)

- Update Process Models

- Enquiry Process Models.

The relevance of each of these products is considered in the next section.

4.4.2 Requirements Specification Products

This section considers the SSADM logical process design products in turn and provides guidance on their use or replacement in an application generator environment. Assuming, from the previous arguments, that the Requirements Specification (ie the Stage 3 product) is inviolate, the question is how much additional design and specification needs to be undertaken in an implementation-independent manner. The precise answer will, of course, vary between environments and should be defined by the supplier in the product interface guide. However, some general principles can be established.

Dialogue design

The Dialogue Structures are produced in Step 510 (Define User Dialogues). At this point they are only a definition of the groups of data items crossing the system boundary. To do more than this would require knowledge of dialogue attributes supported in the physical environment, eg how many colours; availability of 'windows'; size of screen.

Dialogue design is part of the External Design and therefore not necessarily a concern of the implementation-independent specification. Since most application generators provide superior dialogue design facilities, and many use an External Design stereotype as a way of defining the database updates, it is recommended that dialogues be developed using a tool-based, prototyping technique, rather than the SSADM technique. The developers of SSADM recognised that a hands-on prototyping approach to dialogue design was preferable to any paper-based technique, and intended that the dialogue design technique in SSADM should only be used in Stage 5 (Logical Design) if product-based tools are not available.

Update Process Models

Update Process Models (UPMs) are part of the Conceptual Model and therefore part of the implementation-independent specification. However, the production of UPMs is one of those techniques that contain almost no discovery or decision-making. The UPMs can be completely automated in a CASE tool, as discussed in section 3.4.4, being generated from a set of Entity Life Histories, the Logical Data Model and a set of Effect Correspondence Diagrams. If they contain no new information, why bother to produce them?

A UPM serves two purposes in SSADM. It brings together in a single specification all the database processing for a single event, and it forms a design (in the Jackson style) for the update program.

The level of detail and style of specification of UPMs is appropriate for the programs – in general, functions and not individual events become programs, but a simpler view is sufficient for the arguments here – to be implemented directly in a procedural language; they process individual records in sequence rather than sets of data. UPMs specify the conditions governing iterations and selections explicitly.

However, much of the power of application generators derives from their ability to specify processing in a non-procedural manner, either via a 'forms' type interface or a language based on SQL. It may prove difficult to implement the UPMs in the way specified using non-procedural tools. For example, the application generator may infer the read and write statements from the dialogue definition, and the programmer may be unable to control the reading and writing of records – specified explicitly in the UPM – directly. If the UPM structure has no value as a program design, and the program specification can be derived from the UPM's antecedents, it may be that the Stage 3 products represent more appropriate inputs to an application generator.

Unfortunately the optimum specification method varies from product to product. If the application generator is sophisticated enough to include all the features of the SSADM design (the 100% solution mentioned earlier) then the UPMs may be omitted. However, the stereotypes used by some products are limited and may impose unacceptable constraints on the design. Many application generators now include a procedural language for those circumstances outside the capabilities of the declarative languages.

The update processes must be implemented in a way that maintains the integrity of the SSADM design, whilst retaining the productivity benefits acknowledged for non-procedural languages. Therefore the implementation tools must support:

- implementation of explicit state indicator checking to enforce the business rules

- the ability to divorce the database processing from the user dialogue

- commit units at an event level

- specification of update operations against the Logical Data Model, not base tables

- the ability to generate output reports as a result of an update (ie the equivalent of merging a UPM with an output structure)

- a means of implementing the six SSADM models for the death of an entity (instead of the three commonly implemented as automatic relational database functions).

If aspects of the design cannot be supported, then it may be necessary to develop procedural language routines for all or part of the program. In this case the UPM is likely to be required as a framework for the program.

The choice between implementing the 100% solution, designed using SSADM, and compromising some of the non-essential requirements to allow a quicker and cheaper implementation is not only a technical issue. It is the system users who need to decide whether the extra refinement is cost justified. The major determinant as far as updates are concerned is how fully the business rules contained in the LDM and entity life histories need to be implemented. For some simple record-keeping systems it may be acceptable to have the updating constraints imposed by the users, providing they have the required knowledge of the business rules. More complex systems, or those with users who lack business knowledge, will require the business rules to be fully embedded in the software. The difficulties in achieving this in an SQL-based environment is illustrated later in this chapter.

The need for the 100% solution should be examined during Business System Options, allowing subsequent design work to reflect the level of sophistication required. Even the omission of entity life histories (often proclaimed as an SSADM heresy) is acceptable for systems where the user does not wish the system to contain the kind of constraints on updating that results from the technique. However, the decision must be conscious and well informed. Some SSADM projects have produced the 100% design required by the users, and then ignored most of the business rules derived from the entity life histories because they were not explicitly supported in the chosen application generator. Far from being a user decision, these design compromises were being made without even the project managers being aware of the situation.

Enquiry Process Models

Enquiries are generally less complex than updates, and are therefore more readily implemented using stereotype components. Enquiries do not have to check state indicators (although the state indicator may be used as an enquiry parameter), or concern themselves with the complexities of entity death or commit units. It is therefore more probable that non-procedural query languages, and decision-support tools will be able to directly implement enquiry functions.

However, as with UPMs, there will be (product specific) circumstances when an Enquiry Process Model (EPM) is necessary as the structure of an enquiry program that cannot be implemented non-procedurally. Most commonly these are:

- when the output requires calculations beyond the scope of built-in functions;

- when the output format has a complexity beyond the scope of the report-writer;

- when the enquiry uses the same relationship on the data model more than once (in different directions).

The view that a large proportion of system enquiries can be implemented directly, using non-procedural specification languages, highlights a more fundamental misunderstanding about the way SSADM specifies enquiries. Many inexperienced users of SSADM erroneously believe that each requirement identified during analysis becomes the subject of a Requirements Catalogue entry, Function Definition, Enquiry Access Path and Enquiry Process Model. Whilst this view is consistent with the default process model, it ignores the reality that many enquiries in typical commercial systems are either very simple and capable of being specified unambiguously without recourse to Enquiry Process Models, or are decision-support type enquiries which may not be defined in advance of the system being built.

A more practical approach is to classify enquiries, at an early point in the analysis, according to their complexity and implementation method. An appropriate specification method can then be used for each enquiry classification, rather than the default option which will contain unnecessary detail for many enquiries.

Some of the enquiry requirements identified in Stage 1 (Investigation of Current Environment) will be to produce a fixed format output based on known enquiry parameter types, with values for the parameter types being supplied at run-time (perhaps by user or provided by an update function). There will be other enquiry requirements which do not have a fixed input and output format, often referred to as decision-support systems. It is not generally possible to define a possibly infinite series of decision-support enquiries in advance. In most cases end-users will be provided with general purpose enquiry software (eg QBE) to allow them to undertake these enquiries as the need arises. Specific enquiry programs with pre-programmed access to the database are not produced. Such user-defined enquiries are not usually specified other than in the Requirements Catalogue. A typical catalogue entry will define a requirement to support broadly-defined classes of enquiry (with examples), which will almost certainly play some part in specification prototyping. If there is a substantial requirement for role-related data manipulation, facilities may also be provided to extract global data into personal databases.

Chapter 4
Application generators and SSADM design

Enquiries that do have a fixed format can be specified using SSADM and pre-programmed. However, this does not mean that all such enquiries require the production of an Enquiry Process Model and a bespoke program, even in a third-generation software environment. Using generalised enquiry software instead of producing bespoke software is the preferred option for the usual reasons of productivity and maintainability. However, there will be circumstances when the enquiry software facilities will be inadequate (eg for special output formatting requirements), requiring bespoke programs. In practice, the distinction between these two types of enquiry is not as sharp as it may at first appear. For example, the enquiry software may be used to extract a results table from the database, with complex totalling and formatting of output being handled by a bespoke program. Conversely, a bespoke program may be used to perform complex calculations, writing the results to a new table, and then using the standard report-writer to produce the output.

Pre-programmed enquiries are defined in SSADM in one of three styles, depending on the mode of implementation:

- requirements to be satisfied by the use of a parameter-driven query interface (but pre-defined by the system builders instead of defined by users) are defined only in general terms in the Requirements Catalogue, as for the user-defined enquiries

- simple pre-programmed enquiries to be implemented using generalised enquiry software are defined by a Function Definition (plus I/O Structures) and an Enquiry Access Path, but not an Enquiry Process Model

- complex pre-programmed enquiries requiring some bespoke software have a full enquiry specification developed, including an Enquiry Process Model.

These possibilities are depicted in Figure 26.

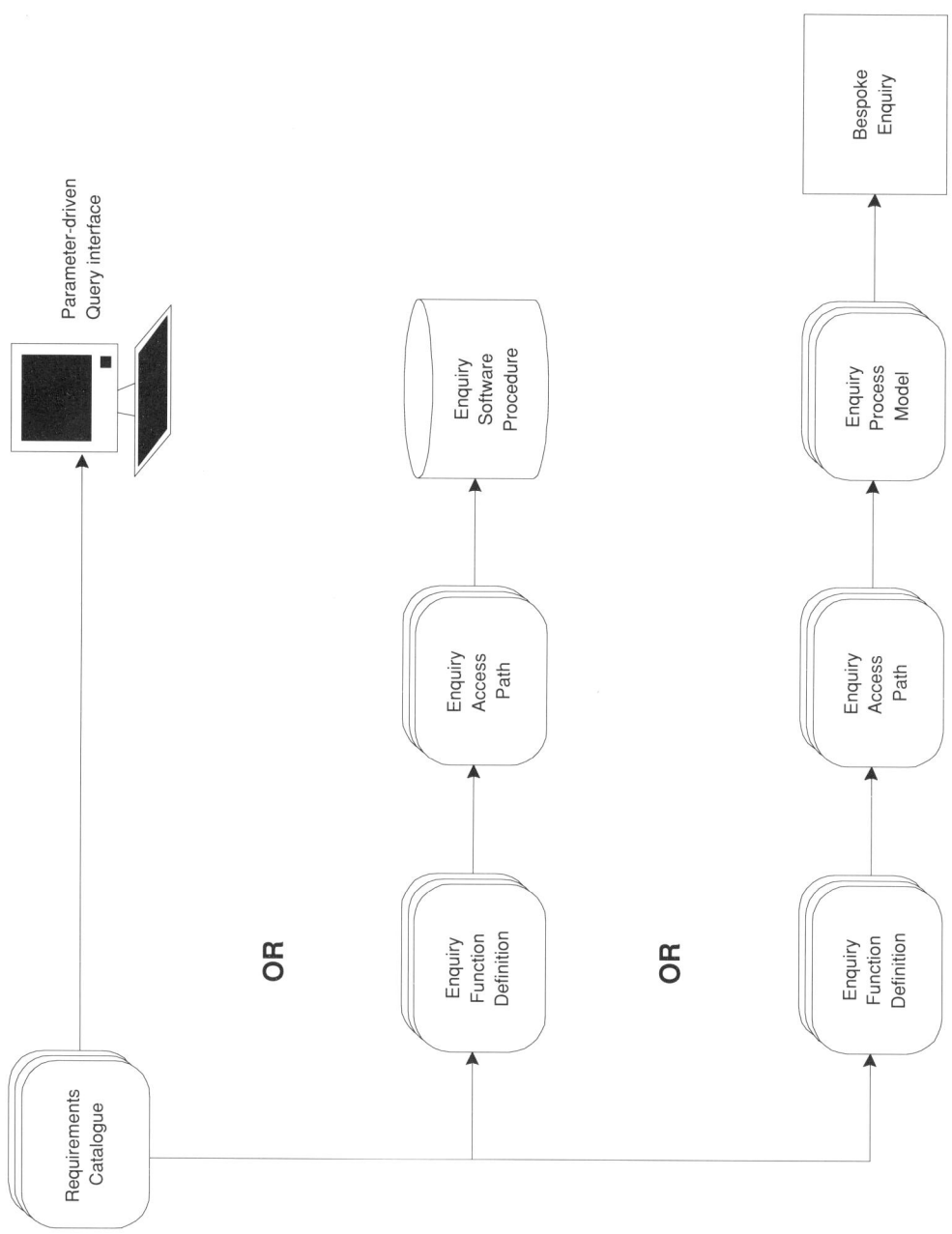

Figure 26: Specification of enquiries in SSADM

There is a significant class of exception to the above guidelines. Some enquiries may be associated with update functions, either as a pre-update enquiry to identify the records to be updated, or a post-update enquiry to produce an output from the update or to investigate an error condition. There may well be duplication of data access for the enquiry in the update. In these circumstances it is recommended that an Enquiry Process Model be produced for the enquiry, enabling correspondence to be established between the enquiry and update structures, and providing the potential for merging the structures, or for program inversion.

It is obvious that enquiry requirements should be classified as early as possible to avoid any propensity to over-specification. In practice the cost difference between providing most of the outputs via an end-user facility, and writing a large number of specific enquiry programs, is likely to be so significant that the implementation style (but not necessarily the implementation products) must feature in the Business System Options.

4.5 Implementing UPMs and EPM: An SQL example

Sections 4.3 and 4.4 highlighted the issues concerning the development of Update Process Models (UPMs) and Enquiry Process Models (EPMs) and implementing them non-procedurally. This section discusses implementing them in SQL and is of particular relevance to the last two of the four key questions identified at the beginning of the chapter.

- what are the characteristics of a function that determine whether it should be coded?

- how are the business rules contained in the Conceptual Model maintained in the implemented system?

Readers requiring more information on SQL are referred to the ISE Library volume: *Database Language: SQL Explained*. It is assumed the reader is familiar with standard SQL.

The explanation that follows is not intended to be a detailed discussion of coding UPMs and EPMs using SQL. Even for application generators with an SQL interface to the DBMS, the use of native SQL by implementors is not extensive. Most frequently the physical processes are specified using proprietary products which map to an extended version of SQL. The purpose of this part is to highlight critical implementation issues that exist for a range of products built around SQL. It describes an interface between SSADM and standard SQL, as a mean of identifying application problems for designers and vendors, which can form the basis for product-specific solutions.

Scope

The primary focus of this chapter is the implementation of events and enquiries, and in particular the relevance of UPMs and EPMs. It is therefore concerned with a limited subset of the Universal Function Model as shown by figure 27 which maps SQL on to the Universal Function Model.

4.5.1 The Universal Function Model

The Universal Function Model (UFM) represents the SSADM view of the implementation components of an update or enquiry function.

Each function is viewed as a series of processes communicating via intermediate data streams. The UFM provides a framework for specifying each component of a function, and for deciding how each of the components is to be implemented in the physical environment.

In considering how the processes and data streams should be implemented, SSADM takes the view that as many as possible should be defined using non-procedural languages and tools. Procedural specifications (based on Jackson structures) are only produced for those components of the UFM that are not easily represented using the application generator definition facilities such as screen/dialogue generators and report writers. An application generator interface must therefore describe how the UFM components can be translated into code. For example, application generators using SQL as the database manipulation language will implement the Process Data Interface as a series of SQL 'views'.

Chapter 4
Application generators and SSADM design

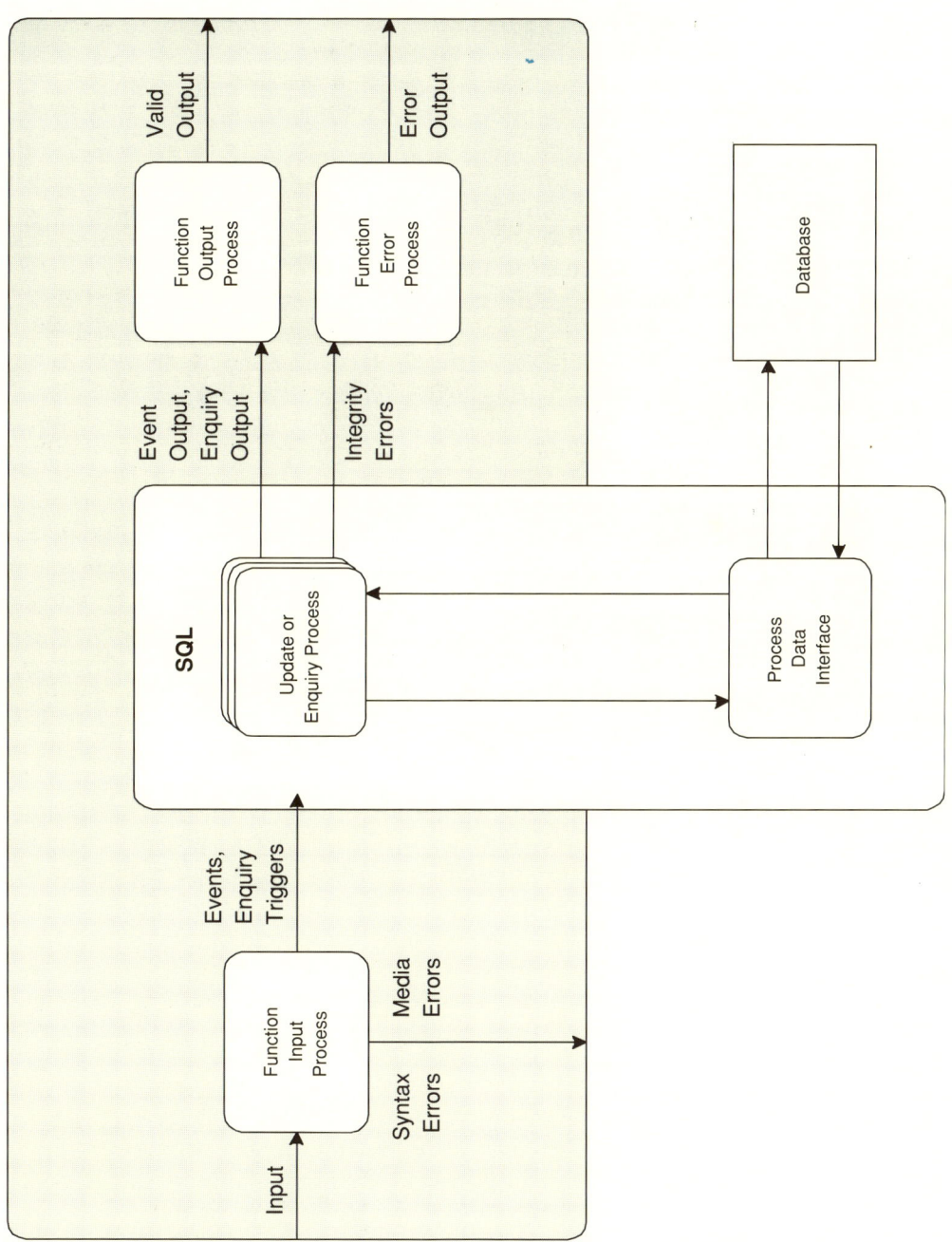

Figure 27: Mapping of SQL on to the Universal Function Model

The conformance of the application generator facilities to the Universal Function Model is a critical measure of the product's effectiveness in implementing SSADM designs. The ability to preserve all the features of an SSADM design in an implementation relies on a close correspondence between the application generator facilities and the UFM components. There may be a direct correspondence between UFM components and application generator components. Alternatively, the application generator function model may contain a different number of components. The latter case is equivalent to the Specific Function Model in SSADM, and the specific model must be described in the interface guide, including the relationship between the specific and universal models. In particular the UFM relies on the processing for system events being specified independently of each other and of the External Design. Some application generators expect the update processing to be specified via the External Design.

The UFM is used in SSADM not only as a representation of the final specification of processing for each function, but as a means of explaining when and how the specification is constructed. It should be clear from section 4.4.1 that interfaces to application generators should not be restricted to a description of how to translate SSADM design products (logical or physical) into application generator code. (Many of the supplier-produced interface guides to SSADM Version 3 were criticised for taking this approach.) Potentially some of the design techniques can be replaced by product-specific approaches. The UFM (or application generator Specific Function Model) can be used to illustrate how the changed techniques contribute to the specification of processing.

4.5.2 Using SQL

In most SQL database products, SQL can be used interactively, via transaction manager interfaces or embedded in host on-line or batch programs. Host programs may be written in a conventional programming language such as COBOL or in a proprietary application generation language.

Some exaggerated claims have been made for SQL's ease of use and its suitability as an end-user tool. Whilst SQL can be used interactively as a retrieval tool, in general the complexity of the language is such that only the most experienced end-users can reliably use the SQL language to interrogate data directly. The explicit use of SQL should not generally be contemplated as an end-user data retrieval capability. Moreover, because of the lack of control available, the use of interactive SQL to update data in an SQL database would not be contemplated as an end-user capability in a system design.

SQL does not provide:

- a means of specifying database integrity errors and the processes to handle those errors

- the format of the valid output from an update or enquiry (other than the default list)

- a means of specifying input data validation

- the user dialogue associated with the input of event or enquiry data.

The use of SQL is therefore generally confined to:

- SQL embedded in a conventional or semi-procedural fourth-generation programming language

- SQL used generically as the basis for defining the data to support a simple proprietary enquiry or reporting tool.

Because standard SQL includes no flow control statements (although a number of the proprietary versions of SQL include this capability), in most applications other than simple data entry, enquiry or reporting, SQL is embedded within another language. If the host language is a conventional language such as COBOL, then the interface is through an SQL CURSOR. The SQL CURSOR definition allows the power of SQL to be used to select the subset of data to be processed; the CURSOR then allows the conventional programming language to read the data one row at a time, similar to processing data from a sequential file.

There are certain key differences between interactive and embedded SQL that have a major influence on how SSADM events and enquiries should be implemented. In embedded SQL, the SELECT statement is replaced by SELECT...INTO, with the INTO clause being used to specify the host program variables to receive the results of the SELECT. Only one row of a table can be returned by each execution of a SELECT. In fact this limitation is the SQL standard for both interactive and embedded SQL. However, a large number of implementations allow the selection of more than one row in interactive SQL. If it is not certain that only one row will be returned, the programmer must use a CURSOR.

Similarly the INSERT statement only inserts a single row into a single table. The DELETE and UPDATE statements both operate in the same way as interactive SQL. Multiple updates and deletes can be achieved with a single statement.

The reason for these constraints is that the developers of SQL intended it for use with third generation languages, such as COBOL or PL/I. They cannot handle multiple rows with single operands. Therefore a mechanism to allow the host language to step through a table one-row-at-a-time was defined – the SQL CURSOR.

4.5.3 Update Process Models

Having established that SQL must be embedded in a host program to work in most useful environments, the question of mapping an SSADM Update Process Model can be considered. Essentially there are two alternatives:

- the host program uses the structure of the UPM or EPM, using SQL to replace the logical reads and writes

- the host program is just a 'start and end shell' with the UPM or EPM mapped to SQL statements whenever possible, and using the UPM/EPM for the structure of the host program only where it is difficult to achieve a direct SQL mapping.

Chapter 4
Application generators and SSADM design

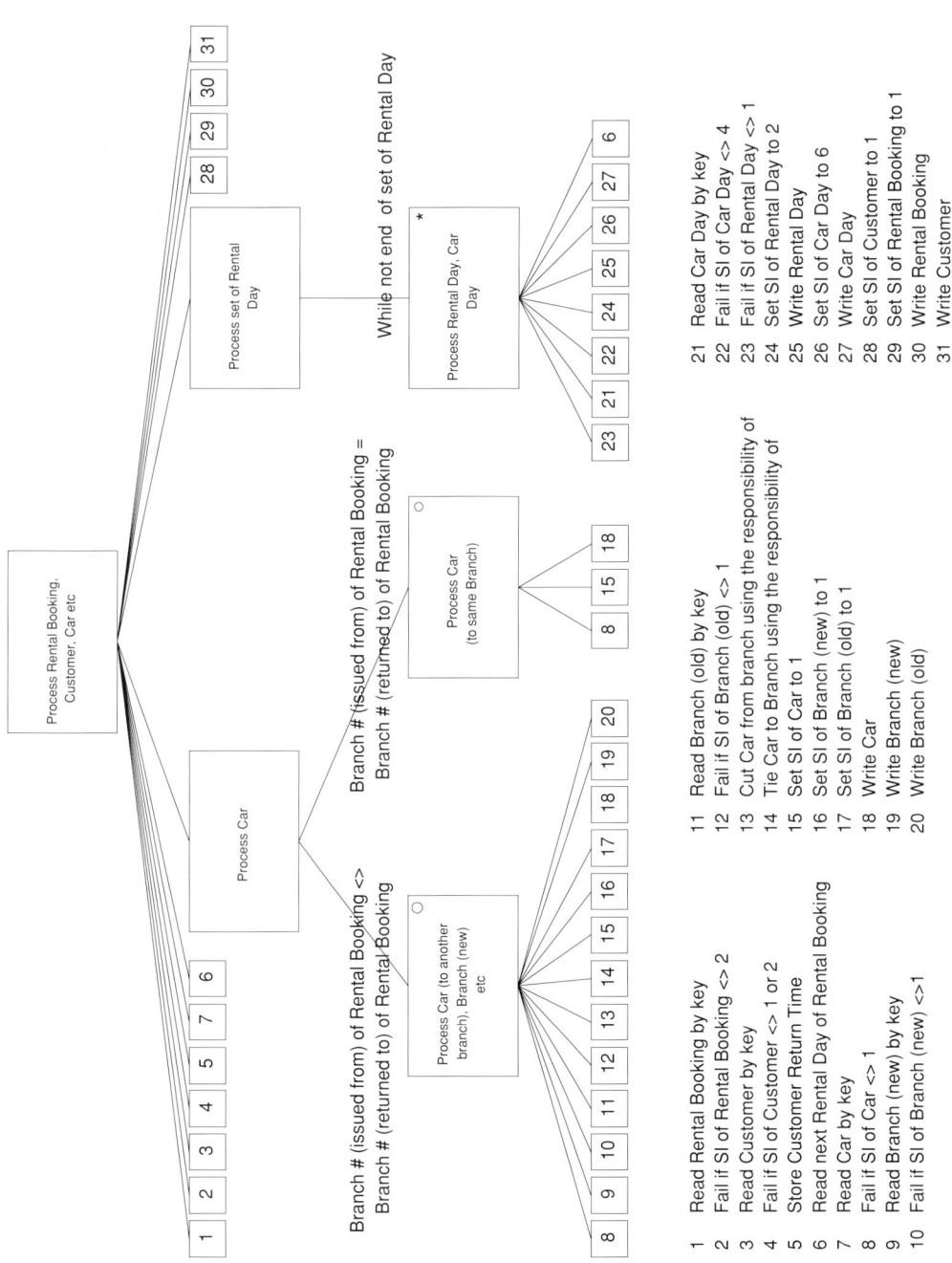

Figure 28: Update Process Model for Customer Car Return

Consider the following simple Update Process Model (Figure 28) for the Customer Car Return event, based on the EU-Rent case study outlined in section 3.4.2 and developed in section 3.4.4.

For simplicity let us examine only the 'Process Set of Rental Day' iteration. In summary the processing is:

- read each Rental Day, checking it is in state '1'

- read the Car Day for each Rental Day, checking it is state '4'

- update the state indicator of Rental Day to 2

- update the state indicator of Car Day to 6.

Converting the UPM operations is not a straightforward translation as SQL statements operate on a set of records not individual records.

Ignoring the structure of the UPM, the SQL to achieve this update (using COBOL as the host language, and omitting assignment statements for clarity) is illustrated in Figure 29.

The UPM includes read and write statements for each occurrence of Rental Day and Car Day. These are not necessary in SQL as an entire set can be processed with one statement, using the WHERE clause. The eight operations and the controlling condition on the UPM have been reduced to two simple SQL statements. Repeated across the entirety of the UPM this seems like a significant saving in coding effort and calls into question the appropriateness of the UPM.

However, some things in the specification are missing from the SQL solution:

- all the Rental Day rows that are linked by a foreign key to the Rental Booking are updated. The specification required the state indicator to be checked to ensure that the Rental Day had not been previously terminated;

```
        EXEC SQL
              WHENEVER SQLERROR GO TO SQL_ERRORS

              UPDATE RENTAL_DAY
              SET SV = 2
              WHERE RENTAL_BOOKING = :WS-RENTAL-BOOKING

              UPDATE CAR_DAY
              SET SV = 6
              WHERE CAR_REG_NO = :WS-CAR-REG-NO
              AND DATE BETWEEN :WS-PICKUP-DATE AND :WS-RETURN-DATE
```

where the host variables are derived from the Rental Booking Entity

```
              COMMIT
        END-EXEC.

              GO TO END.

SQL_ERRORS.
```

host language code to interpret SQLERROR *codes*

```
        EXEC SQL
              ROLLBACK
        END-EXEC.

END.
```

Figure 29: Example update in COBOL ignoring UPM structure

- for each Rental Day the Car Day is updated, although the specification requires the state indicator to have a value of 4 for the event to be valid. An examination of the ELH shows that this omission allows the return of a car to be entered for a rental booking that had been previously cancelled.

The state indicator checks are not defined by the SQL code. These constraints can only be applied by conditions in the host language code. It could be argued that the UPDATE could include the valid state indicator condition in the WHERE clause. Alternatively a pre-update SELECT could be used to identify the rows with invalid state indicators. However, neither are satisfactory. In the first case there is no distinction between an update failure because a record with the specified key value was not found, and a failure because a selected record is in the wrong state. The second case allows an integrity error to be identified, but the update would still need to be conditional on no errors being found, requiring host-language intervention.

The following example in Figure 30 illustrates the coding of the same part of the UPM, but in this case using the structure of the UPM as the structure of the host program, and using SQL to replace the logical reads and writes.

The alternative solutions have been presented here without editorial comment on their correctness or virtue. The choice for implementors is a simple one. If they are required to implement the SSADM Conceptual Model including the behavioural constraints then the UPMs will be needed as the structure of the host language programs. If it is acceptable to implement a simplified version of the Conceptual Model, omitting some of the business rules, this can be as easily done from the Effect Correspondence Diagrams (with added operations), as from the UPMs.

```
EXEC SQL
    DECLARE NEXT_DAY CURSOR FOR
    SELECT CAR_CAR_REG_NO, DATE, SV
    FROM RENTAL_DAY
    WHERE RENTAL_BOOKING =  :WS-RENTAL-BOOKING
```

this cursor define a results table containing all the Rental Days for the Booking

```
    OPEN NEXT_DAY
    FETCH NEXT_DAY
        INTO :WS-CAR-REG-NO, :WS-DATE, :WS-RENTAL-DAY-SV
END-EXEC.

IF SQLCODE NOT = ZEROS OR 100
    GO TO SQL-ERRORS.

IF SQLCODE = ZEROS
    AND WS-RENTAL-DAY-SV NOT = 1
    GO TO INTEGRITY-ERRORS.

SET-OF-DAYS-ITER.
    PERFORM RENTAL-CAR-DAY
        UNTIL SQLCODE = 100

    EXEC SQL
        CLOSE NEXT_DAY
    END-EXEC.

    GO TO END.

RENTAL-CAR-DAY.
    EXEC SQL
        SELECT SV
        INTO :WS-CAR-DAY-SV
        FROM CAR-DAY
        WHERE CAR_REG_NO = :WS-CAR-REG-NO
        AND DATE = :WS-DATE
    END-EXEC.

    IF SQLCODE NOT = ZEROS
        GO TO SQL-ERRORS.
```

Figure 30: Example update in COBOL using UPM structure

```
        IF WS-CAR-DAY-SV NOT = 4
            GO TO INTEGRITY-ERRORS.

        EXEC SQL
            UPDATE CAR_DAY
            SET SV = 6
            WHERE CAR_REG_NO = :WS-CAR-REG-NO
            AND DATE = :WS-DATE
        END-EXEC.

        IF SQLCODE NOT = ZEROS
            GO TO SQL-ERRORS.

        EXEC SQL
            UPDATE RENTAL_DAY
            SET SV = 2
            WHERE CURRENT OF NEXT_DAY
        END-EXEC.

        IF SQLCODE NOT = ZEROS
            GO TO SQL-ERRORS.

        EXEC SQL
            FETCH NEXT_DAY
            INTO :WS-CAR-REG-NO, :WS-DATE, :WS-RENTAL-DAY-SV
        END-EXEC.

    SQL-ERRORS.
```

host language code to interpret SQLERROR *codes*

```
        EXEC SQL
            ROLLBACK
        END-EXEC.

        GO TO ERROR-END.
```

Figure 30 (continued): Example update in COBOL using UPM structure

```
INTEGRITY-ERRORS.

    host language code to interpret    invalid state-variable values

        EXEC SQL
            ROLLBACK
        END-EXEC.

        GO TO ERROR-END.
END.

        EXEC SQL
            COMMIT
        END-EXEC.

ERROR-END.
        EXIT.
```

Figure 30 (continued): Example update in COBOL using UPM structure

4.5.4 Enquiry Process Models

The same arguments advanced concerning UPMs could be applied to EPMs. However, there are key differences between the implementation requirements of UPMs and EPMs. For EPMs:

- state indicator checking is unnecessary;

- query views can be used to (conceptually) simplify the data into a single table;

- SQL may be used to access detail entities directly, rather than via a master entity;

- SQL provides functions (eg COUNT) that eliminate the need for some record level processing.

It is not generally regarded as necessary to check the state of any entity to determine whether the enquiry is permitted. However, the state indicator may itself form part of the selection criteria.

Secondly, it is theoretically possible to create a view for the enquiry which combines all the attributes requested by the enquiry into a single table. This enables the enquiry to be satisfied by a single SELECT statement against the virtual table, typically bringing it within the capabilities of proprietary query-form or report-writer software. This option is not available for updates because views based on a join are not updatable.

In addition to the simplification provided by the query views, SQL can provide a 'short-cut' through the logical access path represented by the EPM. For example, in the Maintenance Booking enquiry described below the enquiry program would not need to access the Branch entity to identify the relevant Car entities.

Finally, SQL provides several built-in enquiry functions that can be used as alternatives to host language coding, further diminishing the role of the EPM structure. The following functions can be included in the SELECT statement:

- built-in column functions, eg SUM, COUNT

- built-in scalar functions, eg INTEGER, DECIMAL

- GROUP BY clause

- ORDER BY clause.

By way of example from EU-Rent; if an enquiry was required to list the number of maintenance bookings for cars owned by each branch, the SQL (omitting the CURSOR which would be necessary to return multiple rows to the host program) is shown in Figure 31.

The enquiry could certainly be coded following the structure of the EPM illustrated at Figure 32 (non-standard operations (numbers 4-6) have been included in this example to make the processing clear) but clearly this would represent a significant over-specification and unnecessary effort.

```
CREATE VIEW JOB_COUNT AS
    SELECT BRANCH_NO_OWNER, CAR.CAR_REG_NO,
    MAINTENANCE_BOOKING_NO
    FROM CAR C, MAINTENANCE_BOOKING M,
    WHERE M.CAR_REG_NO = C.CAR_REG_NO

    SELECT BRANCH_NO_OWNER, COUNT (DISTINCT CAR_REG_NO)
    FROM JOB_COUNT

    GROUP BY BRANCH_NO_OWNER
```

Figure 31: Example SQL enquiry

SSADM encourages the use of generalised enquiry software (including end-user query facilities) rather than the production of bespoke enquiry programs. Different forms of enquiry specification are recommended depending on the complexity of the enquiry, and its planned implementation method. The production of an Enquiry Process Model is only required for a minority of complex enquiries that require the implementation of some part of the function (in terms of the UFM) using bespoke software.

An EPM is likely to be required only for enquiry functions that have one or more of the following characteristics:

- a non-standard output format (eg complex reports on pre-printed stationery) where controlling the format is beyond the scope of the enquiry language/report-writer, and requires manual merging of the input data structure (the access path) with the output structure

- complex calculations beyond the scope of the embedded functions

- complex navigation of the data model, in particular the use of the same relationship more than once in different directions.

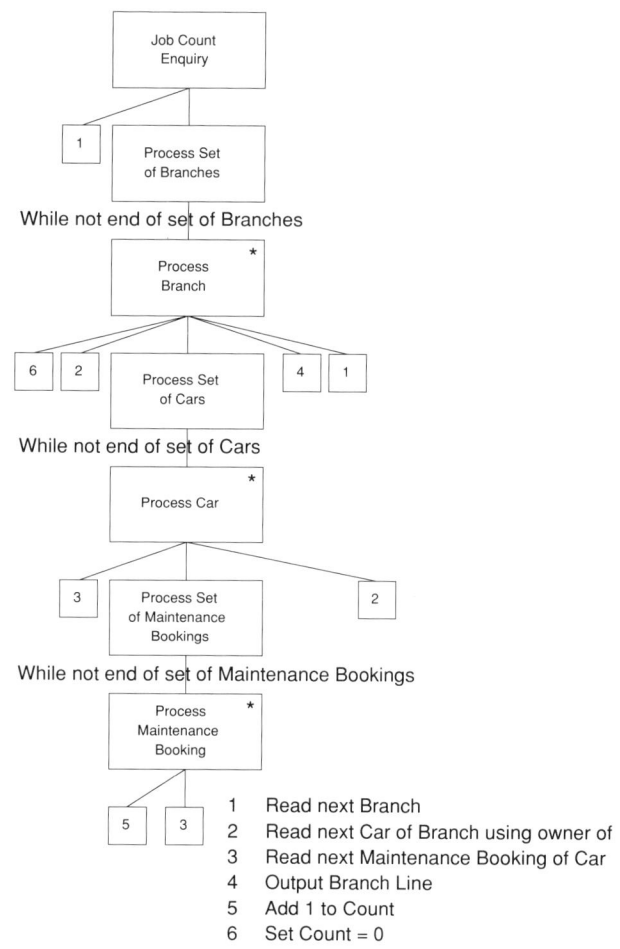

Figure 32: Enquiry Process Model for Maintenance Booking Enquiry

Applying the well established specification principle of 'only specify to the level at which it becomes obvious ...(to the programmer)' it is recommended that the default option for enquiries that are to be pre-programmed should be to produce only an Enquiry Access Path (EAP) to specify the data retrieval elements of an enquiry. (The specification mode of the other components of the Universal Function Model is unaffected by this decision.) Only in circumstances that identify an enquiry as 'complex' (such as the above) should the production of an Enquiry Process Model be considered. Some authorities have suggested that even an Enquiry Access Path presents an over-specification and that the final logical specification for data retrieval should be the 'required view' (SSADM Version 4 Reference Manual, RA-LDM-39). However, the EAP is preferred to the required view for the following reasons:

- the required view does not identify the attributes used as the entry point to the LDM

- the EAP includes selections to process only those detail entities that are relevant to the enquiry, ignoring the others

- the EAP includes sequences of occurrences within an entity type that are not shown on the required view.

The EAP therefore represents a more complete specification for an enquiry than a required view, and the additional effort required to produce the EAP from the required view is minimal.

4.5.5 Conclusions from SQL example

It may appear from this section that the issues surrounding SQL are concerned with the technical details of the most appropriate form of logical specification. In fact the choices are not really for designers or implementors. They are for users.

Many alternative approaches have been adopted by projects for implementing SSADM Stage 3 (Definition of Requirements) products more directly using SQL-based implementation tools, and omitting parts of Stage 5 (Logical Design) and Stage 6 (Physical Design). These range from omitting the production of Update Process Models in favour of Effect Correspondence Diagrams with added operations, to ignoring the defined events altogether and adding processing detail to the Function Definitions. There is little doubt that substantial savings of effort, and hence cost, can be achieved using these approaches. However, the key question is whether these implementations include all the business rules and constraints contained in the Conceptual Model for the application.

As demonstrated above not all the business rules can be easily included in the SQL code without recourse to procedural language extensions. However such extensions may negate the productivity benefits of SQL-based implementation tools. The choice facing the project sponsors is whether they require all the business rules to be implemented inside the system. The less costly alternative is to place the responsibility for maintaining the database integrity on the users of the system (ie the business rules are implemented in the users' heads). The latter may well be acceptable for simple record keeping systems. However, for information systems that seek to control the real world through the Conceptual Model it is essential that the business rules are implemented inside the system.

4.6 Supplier interface guides

The preceding sections discuss the issues that need to be considered when developing an interface between SSADM and an application generator. CCTA, the SSADM Design Authority Board and the International SSADM Users Group Ltd wish to encourage application generator suppliers to develop interface guides to their products. This section summarises the expected contents of the guides.

It is not the intention that supplier guides should provide a direct translation from an SSADM Physical Design. The ability to translate SSADM Logical Design products, or ideally Requirements Specification products, directly into the application generator syntax should be exploited. It is unlikely that the Requirements Specification products will be changed, other than by enhancement, by the interface.

The checklist overleaf summarises questions that SSADM designers will need answered in an interface guide.

Architecture	Can the Conceptual Model, External Design and Internal Design be preserved in the implementation as distinct code. If so, how?	
	Where is the recommended implementation point (in terms of SSADM Stages and Steps)?	
	Which SSADM activities/products is it recommended be replaced by product-specific activities/products?	
	If the interface recommends the production of additional (to Stage 3) design products, what is their purpose, form and content?	
	What are the design stereotypes used by the application generator?	
Process Modelling	How does the Universal Function Model map to the implementation environment?	
	If the application generator uses a Specific Function Model how does it map to the UFM?	
	How do the product-specific approaches recommended contribute to the specification of processing represented by the UFM?	
	How are the business rules contained in the Conceptual Model implemented in the database update processing?	
	What are the characteristics of an update function that determine whether it can be implemented non-procedurally using the application generator, procedurally or as a mix of the two?	
	Can the automatic functionality provided by the application generator stereotypes (eg automatic referential integrity checking) be turned off?	

Figure 33: Checklist for interface guide

Process Modelling Continued	Are commit units defined at an event level?	
	Can the update operations be specified against the Logical Data Model, not base tables?	
	Can output reports be generated as a result of an update?	
	What are the characteristics of an enquiry function that determine whether it should be implemented via end-user query software, generalised enquiry software or requires bespoke enquiry software?	
Dialogue Design	What is the recommended technique for dialogue design, using the application generator facilities to replace the dialogue design technique in SSADM?	

Figure 33 (continued): Checklist for Interface Guide

Annex A: The 3-schema specification architecture

SSADM provides a 'default' Structural Model, containing all the analysis and design activities and products which may be relevant to the development of a large information system. It is a generic approach, capable of being used in a wide variety of project circumstances. SSADM should be tailored to meet the specific requirements of individual projects.

SSADM Version 4 has been designed to allow maximum flexibility. There are many ways SSADM can be adapted for various situations and development environments, for instance, as described in this volume.

In order to ensure that all such guidance is consistent and compatible with SSADM's underlying principles, the concept of a System Development Template has been introduced as part of the philosophy of the SSADM. This template breaks system development into a number of distinct areas of concern. For the purposes of this volume these major areas are (see also Figure A.1):

- Investigation

- Specification

- User Environment

- Decision Structure

- Policies and Procedures

- Construction.

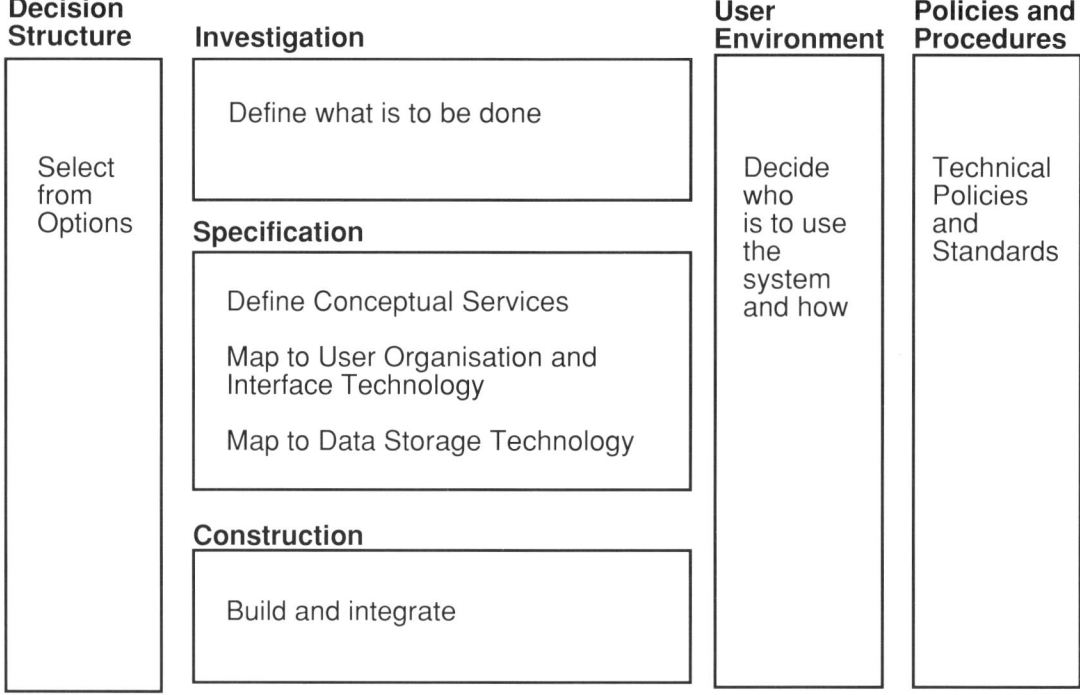

Figure A.1: A System Development Template

The 'specification' component of the System Development Template is further subdivided to contain three important classifications of system products:

- Conceptual Model

- External Design

- Internal Design.

These three parts are collectively known as the 3-schema specification architecture and are described in outline within this annex.

The use of the System Development Template and the 3-Schema Specification Architecture in documenting customised versions of SSADM is discussed in more detail in the ISE Library volume: *Customising SSADM*.

Annex A
The 3-schema specification architecture

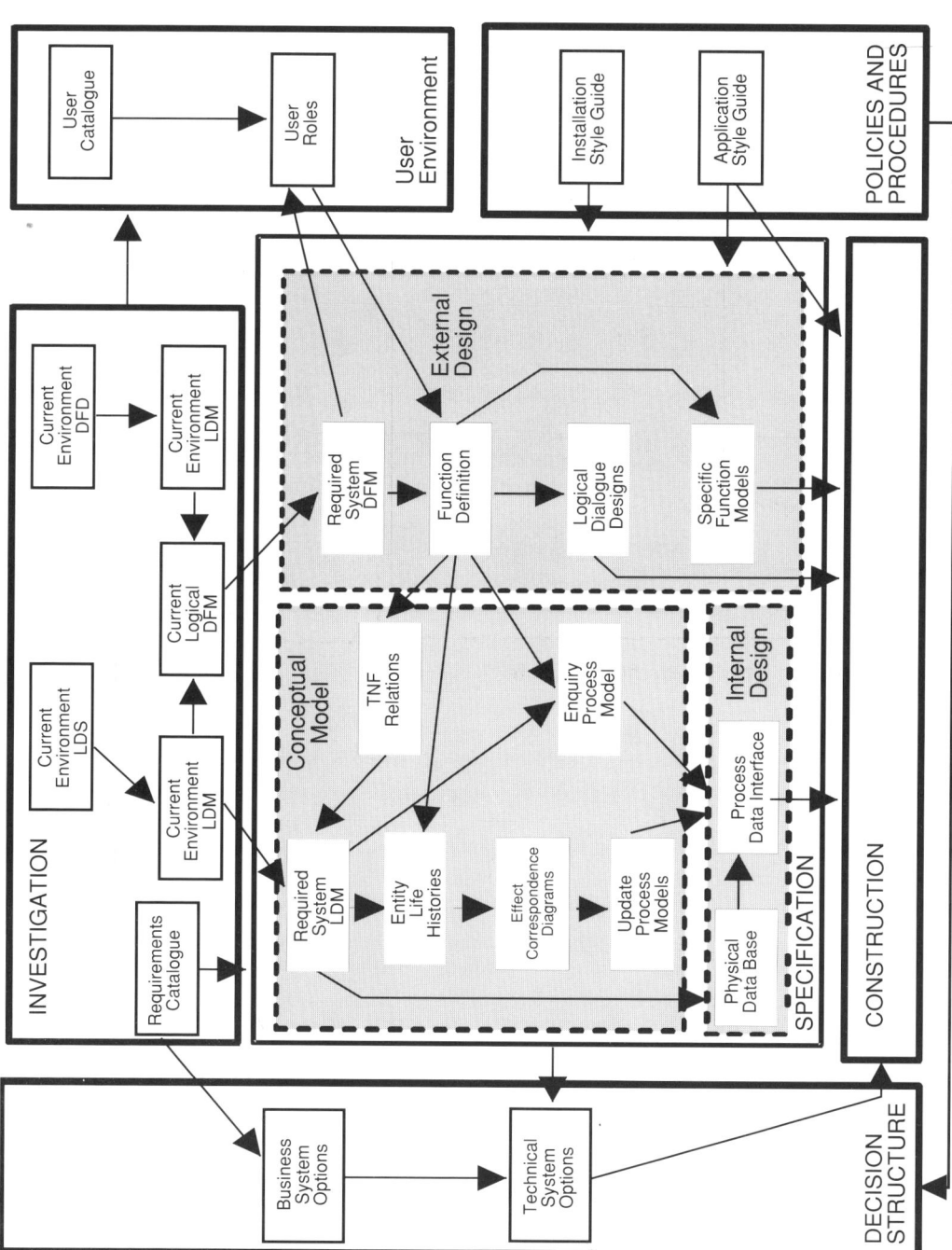

Figure A.2: SSADM Version 4 mapped to System Development Template

The System Development Template and the 3-schema specification architecture

Figure A.2 provides an example of the use of the System Development Template. In Figure A.2 the products of core SSADM as defined in the Version 4 Reference Manual are mapped on to the System Development Template.

The 3-schema specification architecture can be used to divide system specification into three parallel development strands, as will now be explained. The three strands extend the separation of concerns already demonstrated within the SSADM Version 4 Reference Manual via the Universal Function Model.

The Conceptual Model comprises the essential business rules and knowledge, expressed in a Logical Data Model and Entity-Event Model. This is a system model which is independent of the user-interface, and portable between implementation environments. It can be implemented as logical database processes which apparently read and write entities in the Logical Data Model. For the design of the Conceptual Model it is possible to believe that there is in some sense a 'right answer'. Through the use of stereotype components and a disciplined approach to Entity-Event Modelling, the designer can produce a highly objective procedural specification of the database processing. All elements of the conceptual model will ultimately be implemented in the computer system.

The External Design comprises the user interface (data definitions for input/output files, screens and reports; and process definitions for dialogue and batch input/output programs). There are two levels of consideration within External Design: the mapping of business services on to User Roles, and the mapping of these Roles on to the interface technology. The External Design depends on trade-offs between a number of different things (organization structure, ergonomics, system efficiency, end-user input-output device technology, arbitrary preferences of particular users, audit principles, security, user politics, etc.). So any method for designing the I/O processes must be creative, it must involve inventing solutions.

Heuristic approaches such as prototyping clearly have a part to play here.

The Internal Design defines the physical data design (perhaps tuned for performance reasons) and the PDI (elementary data storage and retrieval processes which deal with reading and writing individual records from the physical database, so that conceptual processes can act as though they read and write entities in the Logical Data Model). The Internal Design also depends on trade-offs between a number of things whose relative importance is subjectively defined: time objectives, space objectives, maintainability. Once again, this implies that there is no one 'right answer' and that a heuristic, prototyping approach may be needed.

The 3-schema specification architecture concentrates on those products that will ultimately turn into code. The System Development Template takes a broader view and enables us to identify products which feed into and are developed from those described within the 3-schema specification architecture.

Automating SSADM Projects

Bibliography

Appraisal and Evaluation Library

The Appraisal and Evaluation Library volumes are available from HMSO Bookshops and HMSO Publications Centre. PO Box 276, London SW8 5DT, telephone 071 873 9090 or fax 071 873 8200.

- CASE Tools
  ISBN: 011 330609 1

- Application Generator Environments
  ISBN: 0 11 330604 0

Information Systems Engineering Library

Information Systems Engineering Library volumes are available from HMSO Bookshops and HMSO Publications Centre. PO Box 276, London SW8 5DT, telephone 071 873 9090 or fax 071 873 8200.

- A Guide to the SSADM Version 4 Tools Conformance Scheme
  ISBN: 0 11 330589 3

- Testing Criteria for the SSADM Version 4 Tools Conformance Appraisal Scheme
  ISBN: 0 11 330590 7

- Database language: SQL explained
  ISBN: 0 11 330583 4

- Accelerated SSADM
  ISBN: 0 11 330603 2

- Customising SSADM
  Contact CCTA for details

SSADM documentation

The SSADM Version 4 Reference Manual is published by NCC Blackwell Ltd and is available from NCC Blackwell Ltd Oxford House, Oxford Road, Manchester M1 7ED.
ISBN: 1 85554 004 5

Other publications

Principles of Program Design
M A Jackson
Academic Press
ISBN: 0 12 379050 6

Glossary

3-Schema specification architecture Separates the main concerns of an SSADM specification: the essential business rules and knowledge the system contains; the mechanisms by which the users access the system; and how the logical data model is mapped on to an implementation technology. This architecture is not merely a top-down decomposition of the specification; it also represents a separation of software components that should be maintained in the implemented system (see also Conceptual Model, External Design and Internal Design).

3GL A procedural programming language of a type introduced during the 1960s (eg COBOL).

4GL Usually a non-procedural language packaged as part of an application development toolset.

application generator A software tool which accepts design specifications as its input and from these automatically generates computer applications.

CASE Computer-Aided Systems Engineering

CASE tool Software tool that supports the preparation of systems analysis deliverables (also known as upper CASE), design and construction deliverables (also known as lower-CASE) or both (also known as integrated-CASE).

CCTA Government Centre for Information Systems. A UK government centre which provides advice and support on information systems for UK central government departments.

Conceptual Model In the 3-schema architecture (see Annex A). The conceptual model defines the essence of the IT system – its scope, the information support it delivers and what can happen to keep this information up to date.

embedded SQL SQL statements embedded within a host language, such as COBOL.

entity	Is something, whether concrete or abstract, which is of importance to the area of business being investigated.
event	An event is identified as whatever triggers a process (on a Data Flow Diagram) to update the values or status of the system. An event may cause more than one entity to be changed.
evolutionary prototyping	A similar approach to evolutionary development except that instead of the initial system being refined incrementally, it is replaced by the prototype produced during the next increment of the system's development.
evolutionary development	An approach to the development of an information system in which an initial system containing a reasonably stable core Conceptual Model and a less sophisticated Internal and External Design is refined incrementally to deliver a richer or better system.
External Design	In the 3-schema architecture (see Annex A), the External Design is a mapping of the components of the conceptual design on to:

- User Roles in an organisation, where event and enquiry processing could be packaged differently into functions and functions could be grouped

- the technology chosen for implementing the I/O interface.

fourth-generation language	See 4GL.
Graphical User Interface	See GUI.
GUI	A user interface which makes use of graphical objects, such as icons, for selection of options, and usually has a windowing capacity, enabling multiple window displays on the same screen.
host language	A programming language used in an SQL application to provide control flow and other operations not provided by SQL.
implementation-independent specification	A specification that does not depend on the technology used to implement it.

Glossary

implementation-specific specification	A specification that does depend on the technology used to implement it.
interactive SQL	Use of SQL statements to interrogate data directly.
interface guide	Document showing how to customise SSADM for use with a specific application generator. Ideally produced by the supplier of the application generator.
Internal Design	In the 3-schema architecture (see Annex A), the Internal Design defines the physical database and the process/data interface between the conceptual process and the physical database.
International SSADM Users Group Ltd.	An organisation representing the interests of SSADM user and supplier community.
Jackson Structured Programming	Structured programming philosophy originated by Michael Jackson.
Jackson structure diagram	A diagrammatic representation of a data or program structure.
native SQL	Use of SQL statements without recourse to proprietary retrieval facilities.
non-procedural language	A language where the order of statements is not important, and where there is an emphasis on what is to be done (as opposed to how it should be carried out).
procedural language	A language where the order of statements is important, and where there is an emphasis on how things are to be done (as opposed to what).
rapid application development	An approach to the development of an information system which increases the speed at which a workable system can be delivered by simplifying the Conceptual Model and providing a less sophisticated Internal or External Design.
referential integrity rules	Rules that specify what should happen when deletion and update requests are made concerning a parent – child segment of a data model.

SQL	An abbreviation for Structured Query Language (pronounced 'SEQUEL'), but a misnomer as SQL provides data access and manipulation as well as querying and does not provide the control structures which would be expected of a structured language.
SQL CURSOR	In SQL this is a pointer to a collection of rows that have been returned by the query that declared the cursor. This allows record at a time processing for application programs.
SQL SELECT	In SQL a command that extracts selected rows of a table according to search criteria
SSADM Design Authority Board	A body which advises CCTA on the future development of SSADM.
SSADM Version 4 Tools Conformance Scheme	A scheme for providing an assessment of how well CASE tools support SSADM Version 4. The scheme tests conformance to criteria derived from the British Standard for SSADM (BS7738:1994).
SSADM default model	SSADM as presented in the SSADM Version 4 Reference Manual.
standard SQL	SQL statements based on the international standard SQL 92 (ISO 9075:1992) and which have not been customised for individual implementations.
stereotype component	A 'standard' element in a design which fits a large number of real-life situations.
third-generation language	See 3GL.
view (SQL)	A virtual table that is not physically stored anywhere in the database. It may represent the result of operation on elements or the entirety of one or more physical database tables – eg an extraction of a row(s) or a column(s) or a combination of rows and columns or of a join of one or more tables.

Index

3-Schema specification architecture 10, 63, 64, 99, 100, 102, 103, 107

3GL (*see* third generation language)

4GL (*see* fourth generation language)

Business System Option(s) 75, 79

CASE (*see* Computer-Aided Systems Engineering)
CASE tool(s) 9, 10, 12, 13, 15, 17-21, 30, 32, 35, 38, 40, 41, 43-45, 47-49, 51, 53, 55, 57, 58, 68, 72, 107, 110
CCTA 9, 10, 13, 14, 64, 96, 107, 110
Computer-Aided Systems Engineering (CASE) 9, 10, 12, 13, 15, 17-22, 25-32, 35, 38, 40, 41, 43-45, 47-49, 51, 53, 55, 57, 58, 62, 68, 72, 74, 82, 86, 88, 107, 110
Conceptual Model 63-65, 72, 79, 88, 95-97, 100, 102, 107-109
core SSADM 102

Data Flow Diagram (DFD) 11, 108
Definition of Requirements 95
DFD (*see* Data Flow Diagram)

EAP (*see* Enquiry Access Path)
ECD (*see* Effect Correspondence Diagram)
Effect Correspondence Diagram(s) (ECD) 12, 15, 17, 18-20, 21, 30-41, 43, 45, 48, 49, 57, 58, 72, 88, 95
ELH (*see* Entity Life History)
Enquiry Access Path(s) (EAP) 11, 12, 15, 17, 18, 19, 45-49, 50-52, 55, 57, 58, 76, 77, 94, 95
Enquiry Process Model(s) (EPM) 12, 15, 17-19, 37, 45, 50, 51, 53, 55-60, 63, 69, 71, 75-77, 79, 80, 84, 91-95
Entity Life History(ies) (ELH) 11, 17, 18, 19, 20, 21, 23, 24-29, 30-33, 34, 35, 40, 41, 43-45, 49, 57, 72, 74, 75, 88,
EPM (*see* Enquiry Process Model)
External Design(s) 64, 65, 72, 82, 97, 100, 102, 107-109

fourth-generation language (4GL) 10, 83, 107, 108
Function(s) 63, 67, 73-77, 79-82, 91-95, 97, 98, 102, 108
Function Definition 76, 77

GUI (*see* Graphical User Interface)
Graphical User Interface (GUI) 65, 108

implementation-independent 64, 65, 67, 71, 72, 108
implementation-specific 64, 109
interface guide(s) 9, 14, 63, 71, 72, 82, 96-98, 109
Internal Design(s) 64, 65, 97, 100, 103, 107, 109
International SSADM Users Group Ltd 109
Investigation of Current Environment 76

Jackson 41, 43, 44, 47, 49, 51-53, 65, 73, 80, 109

LDM (*see* Logical Data Model)
LDS (*see* Logical Data Structure)
Logical Data Model (LDM) 11, 17, 32-35, 45, 47, 63, 65, 72, 74, 95, 98, 102, 103, 107
Logical Data Structure (LDS) 21-23, 30, 33, 34, 46, 47, 55
Logical Design 13, 62, 68, 71, 72, 95, 96

non-procedural(ly) 61, 63, 69, 73-75, 79, 80, 97, 107-109

operation(s) 12, 19, 40, 41, 43, 44, 55, 57, 74, 86, 88, 92, 95, 98, 108, 110

Physical Design 12, 13, 45, 57, 61, 62, 65, 68, 69, 71, 95, 96
procedural(ly) 12, 58, 61, 63, 69, 73-75, 79, 80, 83, 96, 97, 102, 107, 109

quits 20, 23, 44

Referential Integrity Rules 109
Required View 17, 46-49, 95
Requirements Specification 68, 72, 96

SFM (*see* Specific Function Model)
Specific Function Model 82, 97
SQL 10, 11, 63, 73, 74, 79-84, 86, 88, 91-93, 95, 96, 107-110
SSADM default model 110
SSADM Design Authority Board 14, 96, 110
SSADM Version 3 82
SSADM Version 4 Reference Manual 13, 15, 18, 30, 31, 35, 40, 46, 51, 95, 102, 110

SSADM Version 4 Tools Conformance Scheme 9, 110
Stage 1 76
Stage 3 68, 71-73, 95, 97
Stage 5 13, 68, 71, 72, 95
Stage 6 13, 61, 65, 68, 69, 71, 95
state indicator(s) 19, 20, 23, 41, 43, 44, 57, 74, 75, 86, 88, 91
Step(s) 15, 18, 20, 21, 30, 35, 46, 51, 68, 72, 84, 97
stereotype(s) 13, 62, 63, 65-69, 72, 73, 75, 97, 102, 110

Task 32
third-generation language (3GL) 13, 61-63, 68, 69, 77, 107, 110

UFM (*see* Universal Function Model)
Universal Function Model (UFM) 80-82, 93, 94, 97, 102
Update Process Model(s) (UPM) 12, 15, 17-21, 31, 34, 35, 37, 38, 40-45, 49, 53, 57, 58, 63, 69, 71-75, 79, 80, 84-91, 95
UPM (*see* Update Process Model)